Mines of the Gwydyr Forest
Part 3.
Parc Mine, Llanrwst and Adjacent Setts

by

John Bennett and Robert W. Vernon

Published by Gwydyr Mines Publications
7 St. Johns Way, Cuddington, Cheshire, CW8 2LX

First Published — August, 1991

© Copyright
John Bennett and Robert W. Vernon, 1991

ISBN 0 9514798 2 2

Printed by Hewitts Printers, Knutsford, Cheshire.

CONTENTS

Preface	5
Acknowledgments	7
Introduction	8
Mineral Lodes and Mine Workings	11
The Setts and the Companies which leased them	19
The Fore-runners to Gwydyr Park Consols	21
Gwaynllifion and Gamfa Fawr pre-Gwydyr Park Consols	22
Gwydyr Park Mine pre-Gwydyr Park Consols	27
Fucheslas pre-1868	29
Cors y Nant	31
Tyn Twll pre-1872	33
Gwydyr Park Consols (Cost Book) 1853-1870	38
Gwydyr Park Consols (Limited Liability) 1870-1874	42
Clementina Mining Company 1876-1883	47
D'Eresby Consols Lead Mining Company 1878-1881	52
Gwydyr Amalgamated Mining Company 1881-1883	54
D'Eresby Mountain Mining Company 1877-1884	56
D'Eresby Mining Company 1884-1889	61
D'Eresby and Gwydir Mines Limited 1890-1891	65
Parc Lead and Zinc Mining Company 1893-1897	67
Brunner Mond and Co. Ltd. 1898-1905	69
C. R. Holmes. Llanrwst Consolidated Mines Limited	72
Watende Limited 1936-1942	81
Llanrwst Lead Mines Limited 1949-1958	84
Methods of Mining adopted at Parc during the 1950s	111
The Parc Mill during the 1950s	115
Department of Scientific and Industrial Research — Parc Mine Experiment 1962-3	123
The Bidston Tidal Experiment 1968	125
Parc Mine in recent years	125
The Mines as they are Today	129
References and Map References	138
Glossary	140

MAPS AND DIAGRAMS

Fig. 1	Gwydyr Forest: Location of main mines.		6
Fig. 2	The Principal and adjacent lodes.		14
Fig. 3	Principal Lessees on Parc and adjacent setts before 1889.		20
Fig. 4	Survey of the Gamfa Fawr mine sett.		23
Fig. 5	Workings in the environs of Parc mine.		26
Fig. 6	Early workings in the vicinity of Tyn Twll.		34
Fig. 7	Mine Setts: 1878 and 1920.		46
Fig. 8	Surface Plan of the Clementina Mine.		48
Fig. 9	Plan of the Clementina Mine: 1883.		51
Fig. 10	Plan of the Gwaynllifion deep adit.		55
Fig. 11	Weighing statistics: Parc & D'Eresby Mine 1853-1884.		58
Fig. 12	Sales advertisements: D'Eresby Mountain and D'Eresby and Gwydir. 1884 & 1891.		60
Fig. 13	Parc: D'Eresby Lead Mine, 1888.		63
Fig. 14	Parc: D'Eresby Mine – 1891. Workings on the Gors Pipe.		64
Fig. 15	Weighing statistics: Parc & D'Eresby Mine, 1884-1920.		66
Fig. 16	Parc Mine: Plan and Section, 1899.		68
Fig. 17	Parc Mine: Surface plan, 1899.		71
Fig. 18	Parc Lead Mine: Surface plan, 1911.		74
Fig. 19	Parc Mine: The Watende Company, 1942- Mill Flow Sheet.		87
Fig. 20	Parc Mine: Plan and Section of Workings on the Principal lode (1910 to 1963).		89
Fig. 21	Parc Mine: Surface plan, c.1956.		91
Fig. 22	Plan showing the more significant workings north of the Principal lode – Fucheslas and Gors.		93
Fig. 23	Parc Mine: Section through the hillside showing main levels.		95
Fig. 24	Parc Mine: Method of Working – 1950s.		112
Fig. 25	Parc Mine: Shrinkage stoping, 1952-1958.		114
Fig. 26	Parc Mine: Mill Flow Sheet, 1953.		117
Fig. 27	Map of Area showing footpaths.		130

PREFACE

Parc mine was the last of the Gwydyr mines at work, and the only one re-opened after the second world war. The last phase of activity, during the early 1950s, ensured that it was the most extensive undertaking, as well as the largest provider of ore on the Gwydyr Mine Field.

This volume describes the development of the Parc mine from its forerunners on the sett, as well as neighbouring minor ventures, in particular at Tyn Twll. This latter sett, home of the Clementina mine, is included in this volume as eighteenth century leases to the Gwydyr Consols and the D'Eresby Consols companies both included Tyn Twll sett, though they are not associated through their lodes.

It was a trip to view the derelict mill at the Parc mine in 1969 that first brought R.W.V. to Gwydyr, while J.S.B. had explored the accessible workings twenty years before that while still a schoolboy.

During the first years after the mine closed in 1956 the timber work and stopes remained in good condition, but years of decay, as well as two earthquakes and a flood have had their effect. R.W.V. last made the trip into the workings in 1990, shortly before the No.3 level was shut off by a concrete choke dam, when he found the mine in a ruinous and dangerous state. No access is now available.

Parc has been devastated above ground as well as below, as it became one of the first of the local mine sites to be fortunate (or unfortunate) enough to be 'reclaimed', for which one might read 'obliterated'. However, sufficient does remain on the ground and in the records to enable us to tell what we hope is an interesting story.

Figure 1 indicates the location of these mines in the overall mining field.

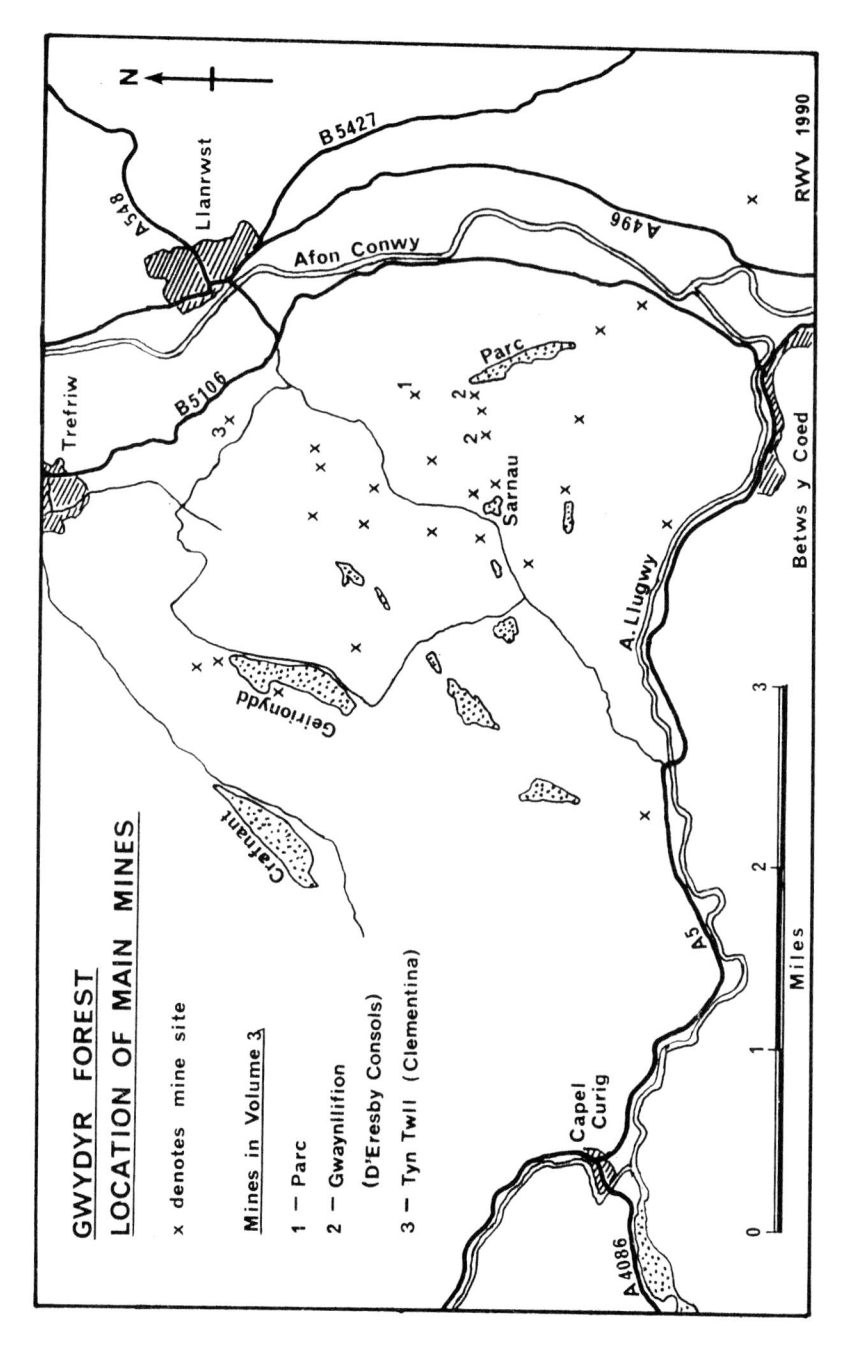

Fig. 1

ACKNOWLEDGEMENTS

This volume covers the most recent phase of activity in the Gwydyr Nant, as well as some early history. That so much material is available for the post-war years is not, sadly, a reflection of the concerned attitudes of the 'proprietors' to preserve a record of their undertaking, but is due to the great foresight of Russell Bayles, who rescued volumes of abandoned papers when Parc mine closed in the 1950s, David Bick, who swept up most of what Russell Bayles had left, and members of the Peak District Mines Society, who finished the job off. We salute these gentlemen.

Elsewhere we are most grateful to Mrs. Peter Gray, who has made available photographs which were taken during her late husbands' spell as Manager at Parc during the 1950s, as well as the original copy of the letter from 'Charlie' Holmes, proprietor at Parc before and after the first world war, from whose writing we have drawn.

Elsewhere we have encountered interest and assistance with articles, photographs, etc., etc., from numerous persons, some whom have already been acknowledged in previous volumes, and some who are acknowledged in the book itself. We are fortunate to have received notes on the local history of the Trefriw area from Mr. T. Arfon Williams, whose family have lived in the area for almost two hundred years.

Others include - in alphabetical order for want of anything better - A. A. Archer, Dr. T. F. Baker of the Proudman Oceanographic Laboratory at Bidston, Dr. Malcolm Howells of the British Geological Survey in Aberystwyth, Owen Pritchard of Llanrwst and Arthur Roberts of Middleton-in-Teesdale.

INTRODUCTION

This volume is the third in a series on the mines of the Llanrwst and Llangelynin Mining Fields, and describes the Parc mine, Llanrwst and minor neighbouring ventures. The Llanrwst Mining Field encompasses both the larger Gwydyr Estate and the smaller Pencraig Estate, which was, in any case, to become incorporated in Gwydyr in the late nineteenth century. The mines in this volume are all found on the original Gwydyr land. As previously explained we propose to reproduce the same short introduction in each publication, to assist 'new' readers to assimilate the general historical background, and we apologise to those to whom it is already familiar. Thus –

In Gwydyr, as is generally so elsewhere, it is not possible to point to the first working or to say just when mining may have begun. As usual in old mining areas there are legends of Roman activities, with the literature being full of mention of Roman rakes, old Roman levels and the old Roman workings. Sad to say, with the possible exception of a small working at Cae Mawr, near to the Roman fort of Caerllugwy, nothing approaching concrete evidence has yet been found.

Even if these workings did exist, they could only have been rudimentary in nature, and no effort worthy of a name was made before the seventeenth century, when the principal local landowner sought to open up and exploit the minerals which were to be found on his Estate.

Sir John Wynn of Gwydyr (1553-1627) could be decribed as the father of the mining which was to take place in the mountainous country surrounding his seat at Gwydyr Castle. We are fortunate that from the Wynn of Gwydyr Manuscripts, which are housed in the National Library of Wales in Aberystwyth, we are able to learn some detail of his efforts.

Sir John had always shown an interest in minerals, but he did not direct any attention to his own Estate until after he had received a letter from Sir Hugh Myddleton in 1607, which asked him to make trial of the mineral waters to be found at Gwydyr. One thing led to another, and Sir John was soon seeking advice from experts about various mineral samples and 'arguments of metals' which he had sent them. The upshot of this was that Sir Thomas Chaloner, who was a kinsman of Sir John and a naturalist of some repute, identified lead ore among the samples sent to him. Sir John then set about obtaining a lease for the lead mines 'on the wastes and commons' around Llanrwst.

Sir John, until his death in 1627, and later Sir Maurice and Sir Owen Wynn, maintained a sporadic interest in the lead mines until the death of the latter in 1666, after which they were neglected for some years. In 1678 Mary Wynn, the heiress to the Gwydyr Estate, married Lord Willoughby D'Eresby, who was later to become the Duke of Ancaster, which was when Gwydyr became part of the much larger Ancaster Estates.

Between 1678 and 1752 the Estate papers indicated that minimal interest was shown by the proprietors in the exploitation of the mines. However, this was to change when Dr. Linden was invited by Peregrine, the 3rd Duke of Ancaster and Kesteven to establish himself on the Estate and seek to develop the mineral resources.

Dr. Diederich Wessel Linden was by profession a doctor of medicine, but was to become an authority on mineral spas and, by his own reckoning at least, on the mining of metals. Between 1752 and 1765 numerous undertakings were in hand on the Estate, often with the advice or involvement of Dr. Linden, and of which much can be learnt from the Account Books of the Agent for the Estate.

During the next sixty years or so there is no continuous record of mining activity in Gwydyr, but there are plenty of stray references to indicate that mining was being pursued throughout most, if not all the period - mostly on the Gwydyr Estate, but also to some degree on the Pencraig Estate. There were usually a number of take notes in issue - short term leases for groups of 'lead mine adventurers' to search for and mine ores - sometimes to local men, sometimes to groups of 'foreigners' from Manchester, Birmingham or elsewhere.

During the early days the Duke was not above taking a financial interest in these ventures, but soon got his fingers burnt, after which he was pleased to let others venture their capital, and take his royalties when they met with success.

The lead ore won was shipped from Trefriw Quay and its forerunners to the smelters in Flintshire as a rule, but occasionally further afield. It does not seem likely that more than a hundred tons or so were shipped in any one year, and probably a good deal less in some years. After 1821 these tonnages were added to by fairly substantial exports of pyrites and small shipments of zinc ore, though still only amounting to a few hundred tons per annum at most.

The pattern of mining during the last half of the 18th century and the first half of the 19th century was on a very piecemeal basis. There were thirty leases in the hands of adventurers in 1838, but only eighty-two men at work, and only one sett employed as many as ten men. 'Mining Adventurer' wrote to the Mining Journal in 1852 - 'The workings on the lodes are generally of a very small scale, wrought only to a depth of eight to fifteen yards, or in some cases about twenty yards from the surface.'

However, Mining Adventurer did go on to remark that promoters in the use of machinery in the development of mines were now coming to Llanrwst. This had much to do with the advent of the Limited Liability Company, which made capital much more easily obtained than previously. This led in turn to the consolidation of small leases to make setts of a worthwhile size to develop, more forward-looking investment of time and money, as in the sinking of shafts, driving of drainage adits, and the erection of machinery, etc. This had resulted by 1900 in over five hundred men being employed on as few as six setts - a very different picture to that in 1838! By 1900 it was principally blende which was being sought, but the employment rate did not continue for very long.

The 20th century saw several commercial efforts digging for both zinc and lead ores, as well as some minor ventures by local men. Parc, Cyffty, Hafna, Pandora and Aberllyn all attracted attention on a much larger scale than ever before, and a good deal of ore was gained. The last episode occurred at Parc, where more ore was being raised in a month during the early 1950s than was being raised from the whole mining field in a year during the 19th century. When Parc was finally left in the late 1950s a long story appears to have come to an end.

MINERAL LODES AND MINE WORKINGS

The mines described in this volume are mainly to be found on the eastern side of the Gwydyr Nant and where the land rises on the western side of the Conway valley to the south of Trefriw.

The Coed y Fucheslas escarpment forms a prominent E-W feature which divides the area into two. To the south of the escarpment, on the High Plateau, lie the Gwaynllifion group of mines, immediately to the north the Gwydyr Parc mines lie in Gwydyr Nant, and further north again lie the small group of mines of which Tyn Twll, or Clementina, is the most important.

This area holds the greatest concentration of lodes in the Gwydyr Forest, the main trend of which is N-S, and many of the earliest workings are found where the lodes became exposed as they crossed the escarpment. A secondary ENE-WSW series were less extensively worked until this century, when the Principal lode in the Parc mine was developed over a distance of one and a half miles. There are several other minor lodes on different trends.

In volume one of this series we included a brief note on mineralisation, and pointed out that the host rock consisted mainly of weak mudstones and harder volcanic rock. The Principal lode was mapped geologically during the 1950s, and the results of this investigation enable us to add a foot-note to the earlier comments - that the mineralisation was governed by the surrounding strata - a fact which had previously passed unrecorded. The essence of the findings was that in the harder rocks the lode dips to the north between 65 degrees and 75 degrees, where is is well defined and carries payable ore, while in the mudstones it flattens to 45 degrees and is poorly mineralised. The Principal lode is discussed in more detail below, but before passing on to this description, the lodes in the southern section of our area of immediate interest will be described.

Looking first at the lodes of the High Plateau, it is obvious from the extensive surface workings – mostly on outcrops in the N-S pattern – that numerous mineral veins cross the area. This is borne out by a late nineteenth century survey of the Gwaynllifion deep adit, a level which had been driven some 1200 feet in a westerly direction from a point close to the northern end of Llyn Parc. A good part of this level had been driven on an ENE-WSW lode, and no fewer than eight N-S lodes were cut in its course, while at least one more was expected to be cut had driving been continued for a more few feet.

John Roberts, who carried out this survey, was quite confident about which lodes these were that had been cut, but as more is learnt by studying the experiences of the twentieth century Mine Captains – especially when the area was re-surveyed by Llanrwst Mines during the 1950s – one has to be a bit more cautious about what is what.

What makes this area problematical is the fact that, after crossing the Coed y Fucheslas escarpment and the Principal lode, at least some of the N-S lodes seem to divide or change their characteristics. However, what can be said is that the lode which was picked up by the Gwaynllifion deep adit was known during the nineteenth century as Sutton's lode, while the most significant N-S lodes which it cut were the Red lode (Gors lode in Gwydyr Parc), Owen's lode (Fucheslas lode in Gwydyr Parc) and the New lode, on which the engine shaft was sunk during the 1870s.

What must be taken as the definitive survey of the Gwaynllifion deep adit and workings was made during the 1950s by Llanrwst Mines Ltd., by which time it was being described as the Alltwen (Park Lake) adit. A map of the workings appears in Figure 10, to be found in the chapter which discusses the development of this sett, but it is a useful reference to the following description and adjunct to any discussion of the lodes in this area.

The first 600ft. of the level - generally westerly in direction - were not actually driven on any mineral vein. This is unusual in Gwydyr in the 1850s -the date the level was started - and must be one of the earliest levels driven solely for development of a mine in this area. In most cases the old men were only content to drive along a vein, even when they were seeking to reach a particular spot.

The level did cut a 6in. pyritic vein after 400ft. driving, and this had been driven on to the north for about 100ft. Initially this had been considered to be the southerly continuation of the Gors lode, but it was subsequently found not to be so, and was a lode which had otherwise been unrecorded.

Some 300ft. beyond this intersection a second lode was cut, again about 6ins. in width, and in which blende was the predominant mineral. This proved to be the southerly extension of a part of the Gors lode, which had split to the south of the the Principal lode, and was driven on for a short distance to the north.

Beyond this the deep adit was driven west on what Llanrwst Mines survey described as a blende stringer. This had been known during the days of the nineteenth century proprietors as Sutton's lode, which may be assumed to be an easterly extension of the Old Alltwen lode, which was described in the first volume of this series on the Gwydyr mines. At the end of this run along Sutton's lode the deep level cut another lode of some significance - having cut three minor N-S lodes in the meantime.

The more important lode which had been reached here was the southerly extension of the Fucheslas lode, known in this sett during the early days as Owen's lode, and it was responsible for displacing Sutton's lode some distance to the south. Owen's lode was some 3ft. to 5ft. in width at this place, and contained good values of lead ore and blende. The lode was driven on to some extent in the deep adit, both to the north and to the south, as they sought the E-W lode on which they had been previously driving. There were extensive surface workings on Owen's lode to the north of the intersection with Sutton's lode, on the southerly end of which Owen's shaft had been sunk.

After travelling some 50ft. south on Owen's lode the deep adit turned WSW, when, after a further 200ft. or so driving it intersected the New lode. This intersection had been chosen during the 1860s as a beneficial spot to sink an engine shaft to the deep adit, and what used to be Rawson's shaft was extended to achieve this object - it also came to be known after that as Sutton's shaft, to commemorate the chairman of directors of that day.

Beyond the New lode the deep adit continued WSW for about 200ft. more, at which point the Llanrwst Mines surveyors found it blocked by a fall. The evidence from the Mine Captains reports made when it was first being opened up suggest that they had expected to be under Cobbler's lode by that juncture, but there is no evidence that they had found anything worth reporting. Beyond this there was no driving west, but it does seem very probable that the lode identified as Sutton's lode corresponds to the Old Alltwen lode, which was described further to the west as mentioned above.

In the Nant Gwydyr the Shale, Gors and Fucheslas lodes were the most important N-S lodes, though the former held no significant ore in this sett, and was only subject to a minor trial in the Cilstent mine in the early days. Even so, it has a good deal of significance for the area as a whole, being an extensive shear zone comprising crushed black shale with patches of calcite and quartz. It is impregnated with blende, but does not become well mineralised until a few miles to the south, where it was worked extensively in the Aberllyn mine. In the old Parc workings it has been driven on for 250 feet,

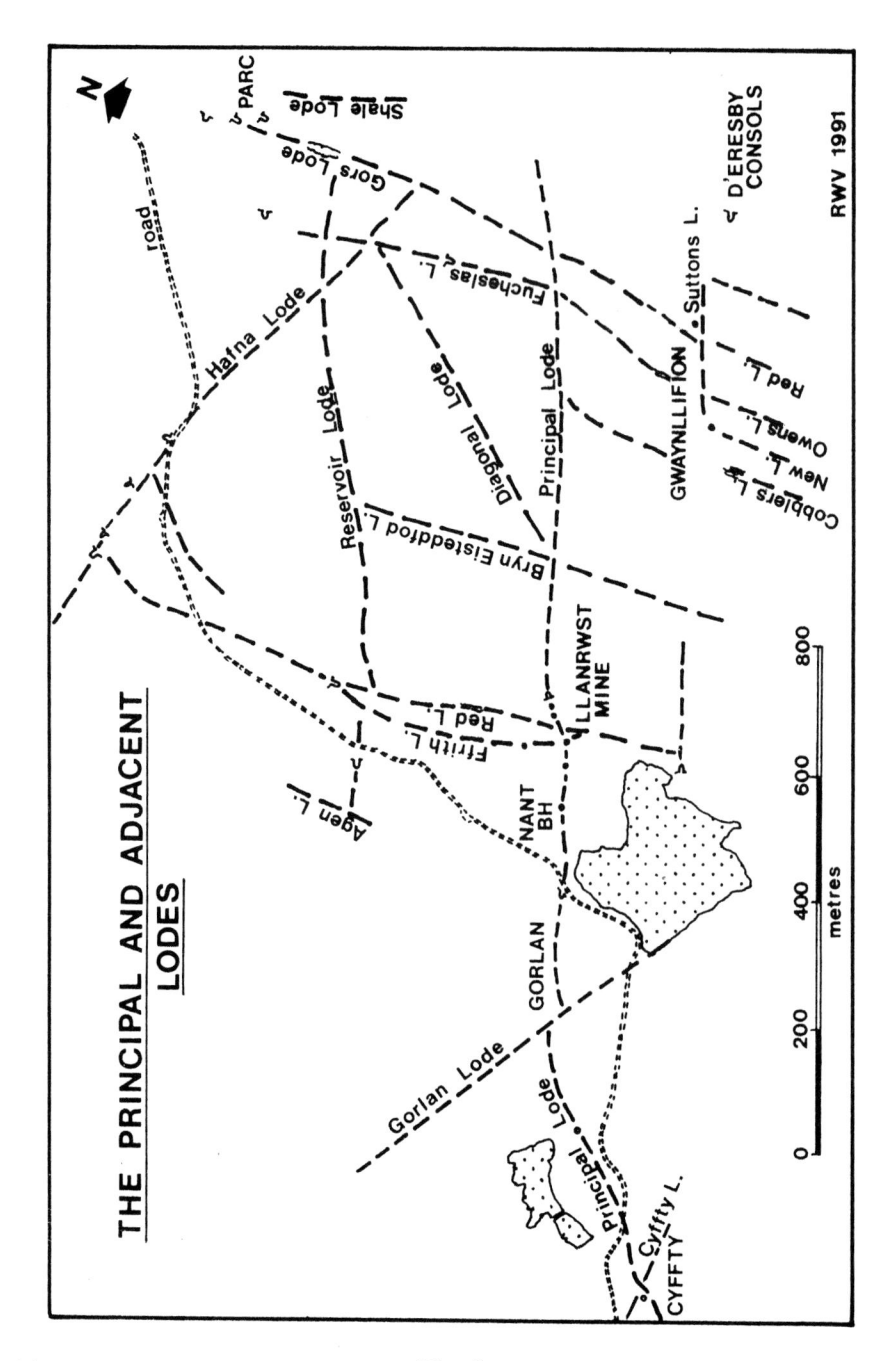

Fig. 2

where it seems that the old men lost the nearby Gors lode for a time. Perhaps its greatest significance in Parc is that it cuts off the Principal lode at its eastern end.

The Gors lode, which is one of the major lodes in the Parc mine, lies to the west of the Shale lode, and may, in some instances, come close enough to merge with it. While it has been recorded as up to thirty feet in width it is more usually between three and a half and four and a half feet. The matrix of this lode is usually quartz, containing predominantly galena, though with some blende.

Substantial mineralisation continues at depth to 500ft below the collar of the New shaft, which was sunk during the 1880s on the 'Gors pipe', the deepest workings in the Gwydyr Forest. A second shaft on this pipe of ore, the Gors shaft, was sunk alongside the New shaft at the same time, and reached 510ft.

The Gors lode workings were also served by the No.5 level, originally an ancient mine which appears to have started from an adit on the Fucheslas lode well down the valley and then swung onto the Gors lode in the region of the No.4 level adit.

During the last years of mining in Parc the Gors lode was driven south from the Principal lode on two levels, but was left when it split into three and became ill-defined and impoverished. As mentioned above, there are early workings on the High Plateau on the outcrop of the Gors lode after it crosses the Coed y Fucheslas escarpment, and where it becomes known as the Red lode.

The Fucheslas lode, which lies to the west of the Gors lode, attracted a good deal of attention in the early days, being worked at surface on the escarpment, and extensively on the outcrop on the High Plateau, as mentioned above, and where it was known in the latter instance as Owen's lode. It generally varied between 3ft. and 5ft., and carried both galena and blende, but was not thought of as highly as the Gors lode.

Before the 1860s no workings were carried out below the level of the deep adit, which commenced near the Parc Villa, though at that time a level was driven across from the Gwydyr Park mine, in the area of Kneebone's Cutting, to cut the Fucheslas lode some fathoms deeper than the Fucheslas deep adit. They proposed to drive south on the Fucheslas lode, when they found it, and hoped for good results at the junction of the Fucheslas and Diagonal lodes, which had already provided good ore at a shallow depth in Harker's mine and from Johnnies shaft. Unhappily this did not prove to be the case, though the Fucheslas lode was explored for some distance in this level.

The positions of the Principal lode and adjacent lodes are shown in Figure 2, while detail in respect of the workings on these lodes is found in Figure 20. This figure appears in the later chapter, in which the Parc mine is described during its last phase of work during the 1950s. Similarly the somewhat complex picture of the development of the Gors and Fucheslas lodes, including nineteenth and twentieth century efforts, is shown in more detail in Figure 22 in the same chapter.

The Principal lode - trending ENE-WSW and up to 12ft. in width - was the scene of the most extensive working in Gwydyr, most of which took place during the twentieth century.

Prior to that minor efforts on the lode had been made on the Llanrwst, Gorlan and Cyffty setts, while it had also been discovered in the Parc mine levels at the very end of the nineteenth century - at which time it had not excited interest. However, it became the focus of attention for all the later proprietors of the Parc mine, especially after the second world war, when a national drive to revive the mining industry, high metal prices, and the new technology which enabled lower grade ores to be worked profitably, led to the most important episode in the history of the Parc mine.

The important points of access to the Principal lode, on the intersection with the Fucheslas lode on the No.2 level, and the intersection with the Gors lode on the No.3 level, had both been achieved over fifty years before Llanrwst Mines Ltd. began their major development of the mine, and their predecessors had already driven on and stoped the lode to quite some extent.

To the east it had already been established that the Principal lode was cut off by the Shale lode, so marking off the easterly boundary of the mine.

To the west the No.3 level had been at least partially stoped to within 350ft. of the intersection with the Bryn Eisteddfod lode, while the level itself was driven some 560ft. beyond the last of the stopes. The description which was given to it at this time, of being a very strong lode with very little sulphide mineralisation, was not much encouragement to Llanrwst Mines, but, with their more sophisticated methods of extraction, they evidently thought that the game was going to be worth the candle.

The No.3 level was the main haulage level, and, as can be seen from the plan of the workings in Figure 20, it was to be extended so far as to get under the Cyffty mine before Llanrwst Mines finished on the sett - in the region of 8000ft.

As can be seen in the plan and section, No.2 level did not quite reach the extent of the No.3. It had been driven some 650ft. west of the intersection with the Fucheslas lode when Llanrwst Mines embarked on their phase of operations in 1958, and had been driven a good deal further before they finished.

Although the Principal lode is generally described as trending ENE-WSW, there are some variations to this rule. For example, between the Bryn Eisteddfod lode and Llanrwst mine the lode swings slightly to the north and then sharply to the south towards the Llanrwst crosscourse, where it exhibits a NE-SW alignment.

West of this point it resumes its normal trend until it intersects the Gorlan lode, after which it once again assumes a NE-SW line until it reaches Cyffty. In several places the Principal lode has split into two, or has a secondary lode running alongside it - such a lode was followed briefly in the No.2 level, and, when it was realised that they were not on the main course, the men christened it the 'Mugs' lode.

From the point that the Principal lode intersects the Gorlan lode, and on westwards to Cyffty, there is a change for the worse in mineralisation. The lode became poorly defined, with evidence that it was starting to split, and with increases in unwanted quartz, calcite and marcasite. The last plans made in this area suggest that the men were, in fact, having to search for the lode.

The No.2 level drivage also ceased hereabouts, at a point that the Cyffty 10 fathom level had been intersected, suggesting a similar dissatisfaction with the state of the lode.

Elsewhere during the 1950s the proprietors sunk the Parc underground shaft in the vicinity of the intersection of the Principal lode and the Gors lode, with the object of studying the Principal lode in depth. In the event only half of the planned 500ft. were sunk, as the No.4 and No.5 levels driven from this shaft indicated that the lode progressively deteriorated in depth. The No.5

level was driven 160ft. to intersect the lode, which was described at that point as comprising barren stringers. The results of several boreholes drilled from the shaft gave no encouragement, and it was consequently abandoned. Inclined shafts were sunk at intervals below the No.3 level,but these were no more successful in uncovering payable ore, and none were stoped.

The N-S lodes which intersected the Principal lode had the effect of displacing it - the Llanrwst crosscourse 240ft. to the south, the Gorlan lode 170ft. to the north. Several of these lodes were tried at their intersections. The Gors lode was driven south on both No.2 and No.3 levels, but was found to split and exhibit poor mineralisation; the Bryn Eisteddfod lode was followed 330ft. south from the No.2 level, but was found to consist primarily of saccharoidal quartz. This last vein was christened the 'Red Water' lode by the miners, on account of the red stalactitic limonitic deposits which were carried into the drivage by the mine water. Only the Gorlan lode raised hopes, when good ore values were found near the intersection with the Principal lode, but these were very localised.

It would appear, then, that the best ore in Parc mine occurred at the eastern end of the lode, where there is a high intensity of intersections with N-S coursing lodes, and where the mineralisation controls are most favourable. This may be enhanced by the number of E-W, or diagonal lodes which are found in this section of the mine, including in particular the Reservoir lode, the Diagonal lode and the Hafna lode.

The Reservoir lode, which lies parallel to the Principal lode, and some 1200ft. to the north, is from 6ins. to 2ft. in width, and is composed primarily of saccharoidal quartz disseminated with galena, together with bunches of calcite and blende. This vein is intersected by the Hafna lode a little to the west of Kneebones cutting.

The Hafna lode in this area is actually split into two, the southern branch being a thin stringer, but the northern branch well defined. It has been driven on for some 1200ft. north-west from the intersection, and shows improved values in the region of the intersection.

The third cross lode is the Diagonal lode, which trends NE-SW, though this is the least important of this group. However, at its intersection with the Fucheslas lode there is an enriched area which attracted attention many years ago, and at which point 'Johnnie' Harker's shaft has been sunk.

At the Tyn Twll mine the most important workings were carried out on an E-W lode, which ran in the line of the Roadside shaft and the later Engine shaft, and on a N-S lode which intersected the E-W lode in the region of the Engine shaft. The relationship between these two lodes and the N-S lodes in the adjacent Parc mine sett or E-W lodes in the setts to the west have never been determined. The easterly workings suffered badly from flooding, as they underworked the alluvial deposits of the nearby river valley.

There were several other minor lodes - indeed, the hillside was once described as being 'seamed with workings' - and some of these must have been very old in Gwydyr terms. However, none of them was of any great significance.

THE SETTS AND
THE COMPANIES WHICH LEASED THEM

Figure 3, on the next page to this, lists the principal early workings on that area of the Gwydyr Estate which we are discussing in volume three. It illustrates how the smaller leases were drawn together by larger proprietors to form companies, and how these companies came and went in the area. It is possible to draw a line of a sort with the formation of the two Gwydyr Park Companies, the first of which was a Cost Book Company formed in 1853, and the second a Limited Liability Company formed in 1870. These two finally incorporated all the principal setts in this area of the Estate, with the exception of Cors y Nant, which was eventually included in the lease of one of the more significant companies to succeed Gwydyr Consols on this ground.

However, while Gwydyr Park Consols drew these various points of work together under one management, they did not long remain so, and the lower half of Figure 3, indicates the fate of the various components when they ceased to be consolidated. In the first instance, then, we will look at the lesser ventures which went to make up the Gwydyr Park Consols Companies, secondly examine the history of the two 'consolidated' companies, and then follow the fate of their offspring, one of which, the future Parc mine, was to dwarf all its forerunners.

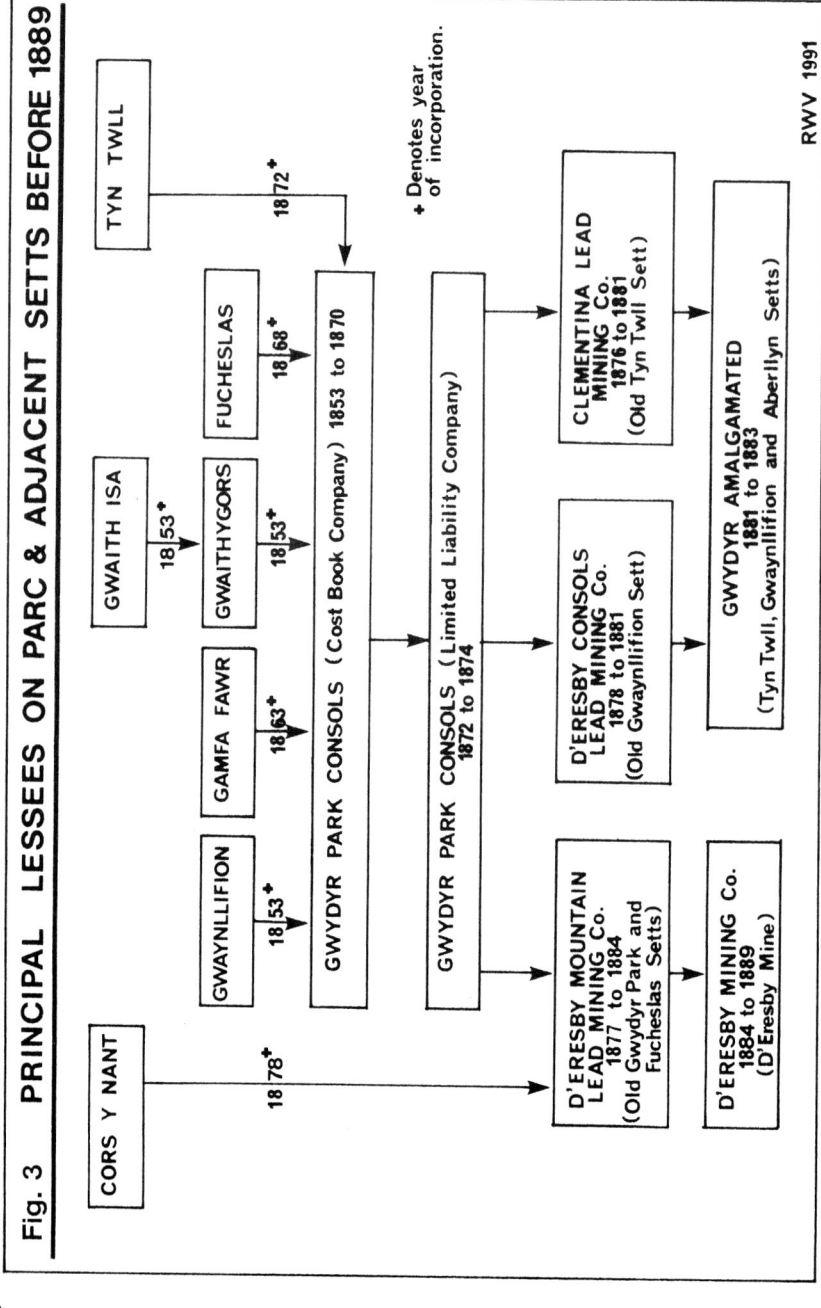

Fig. 3 PRINCIPAL LESSEES ON PARC & ADJACENT SETTS BEFORE 1889

20

THE FORERUNNERS TO GWYDYR PARK CONSOLS

The first Gwydyr Park Consolidated Mining Company was formed in 1853, when they obtained the leases of the Gwaith y Gors and Gwaynllifion setts, to which they subsequently added Gamfa Fawr, Fucheslas and Park Gate, or Parc yr Hisglog, as it was subsequently described. It was the second Company in 1870, who added Llety & Tyn Twll to their property. Although the Gwydyr and Gwaynllifion setts only amounted to forty-two acres, and the Tyn Twll and Llety setts to thirty-two acres, they embraced all the principal sites of activity on this part of the Estate during the time that the two 'Consols' Companies were at work.

Before describing the earlier ventures on these setts, it is interesting to go forward a few years to hear how the Gwydyr and Gwaynllifion areas, at least, were described in the Watson Brothers' Mining Circular in 1877, when the Watsons, who were billed in the Mining Journal as 'Mineowners, Stock and Share Dealers, etc.', were seeking to awake the interest of investors in these mines. By then they had renamed this area D'Eresby Mountain, when the Gwydyr sett became the D'Eresby Mountain mine, and Gwaynllifion became D'Eresby Consols mine.

> They wrote: *These mountains through which we are climbing are riddled with old shafts, and scored in all directions with adits and open cuttings of the old miners; so that, while stopping to admire the grandeur of any particular spot or bit of scenery around, we are likely, if we step back without thought, to drop into an ugly and awkward hole. But these old works and excavations and adits show the great extent to which primitive mining was carried on some years ago in the district, and the riches which must have been obtained to enable the work to be done. In one spot, in D'Eresby, we found the remains of some primitive smelting works, and from the shallow workings on this mountain many hundreds of tons of lead ore were obtained.*

This was a picture which could be painted for much of the Gwydyr Forest at that time - a decidedly piecemeal approach to the business of raising the lead and zinc ores which were to be found, with many workings which did little more than scratch the surface. However, one aspect of Watsons' description did set D'Eresby Mountain aside from other parts of the Forest, and that was his mention of smelting-works - of which more anon. These were most probably on the Gwaynllifion sett, which is the first we will describe, along with the adjacent Gamfa Fawr.

GWAYNLLIFION AND GAMFA FAWR PRE-GWYDYR PARK CONSOLS

Gwaynllifion and Gamfa Fawr both lie in the southern-most part of the area which we are considering in this volume, being wholly in the Betws-y-Coed Parish, on what used to be described as the High Plateau. On the High Plateau setts a significant part of the operations were devoted to the same N-S coursing lodes which will be described in the adjoining Fucheslas and Gwydyr Park setts to the north of the High Plateau, though the name of the lodes always changed when it crossed the boundary, which can lead to some confusion!

It is not known whether this part of the Estate attracted any attention during the first recorded period of mining activity in Gwydyr, when the Wynn family sought to develop the mineral potential during the first half of the seventeenth century. However, an entry in John William's Account Book for the Gwydyr Estate, dated November, 1752, makes reference to payments to Dr. Linden towards erection of an Assay Furnace at 'Upper Gwydir'. (As mentioned previously John Williams was the Gwydyr Agent for the Ancaster family of Lincolnshire, Gwydyr having become an appenage of the extensive Ancaster Estate when the Gwydyr heiress married Lord Willoughby D'Eresby in 1678. Dr. Linden was the 'mining consultant' employed by the 3rd Duke of Ancaster during the 1750s and 1760s to assist in his mining ventures in Gwydyr.)

We do know that Sir John Wynn was smelting ore somewhere on the Estate in 1621, but the mention of smelting works in 'Upper Gwydir' in William's accounts seems to make it likely that, rather than being those of Sir John, these were the ones which the Watsons discovered. Linden spent £3.12s.0d. on the construction - equivalent to several weeks work by a skilled mason - which suggested something sufficiently substantial to have lasted in some form until 1878. However, there is no evidence that Linden met with any success in his smelting, which was probably a short-lived exercise.

Whether the so-named 'Gwydir ore' which contributed to the total ore weighings for Gwydyr Estate in 1753 came from the workings on the 'High Plateau' can only remain a matter of conjecture. There can be no doubt that lead ore was raised from time to time, if not continuously, from the extensive surface and shallow workings on the 'High Plateau' setts, as well as their neighbours, during the second half of the 18th century. However, as has been

Fig. 4

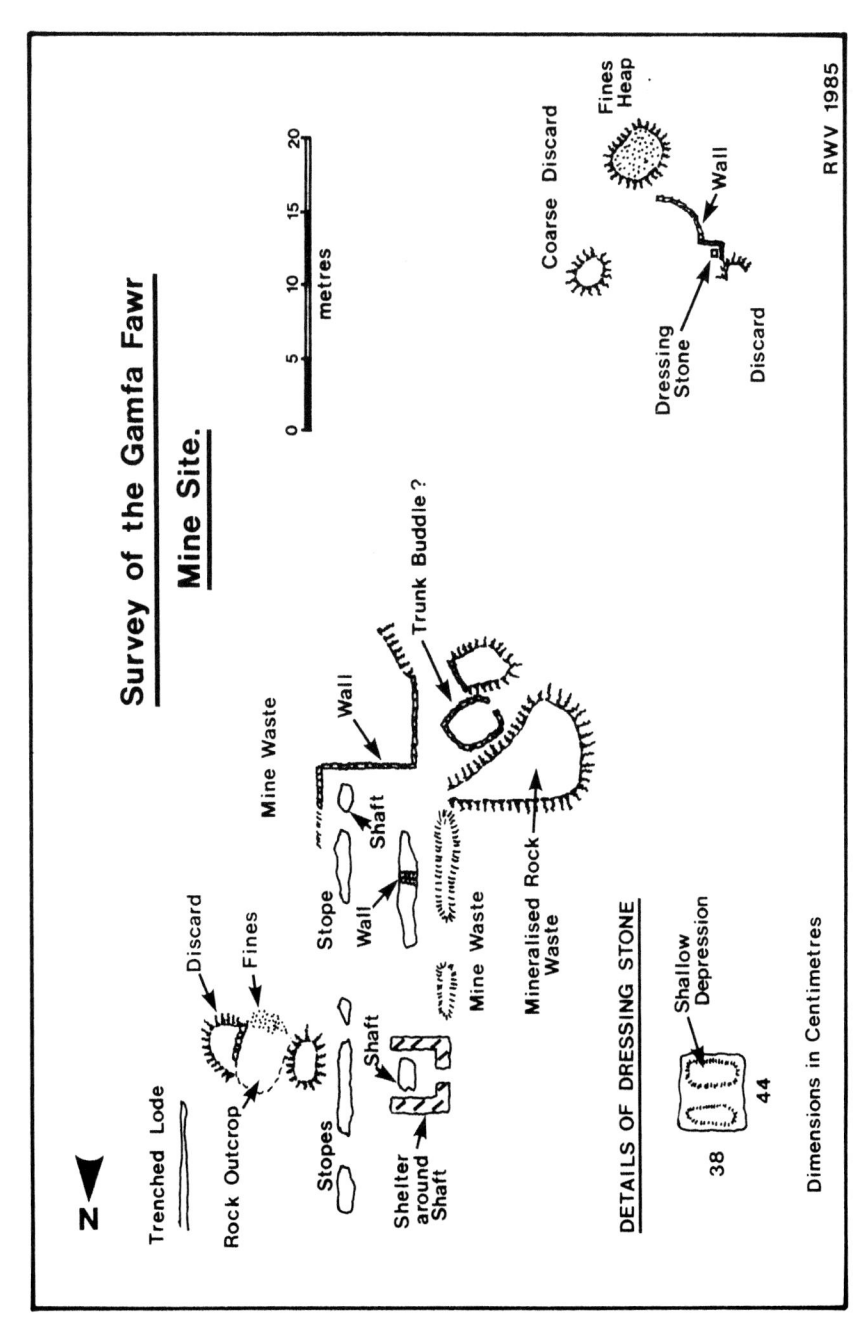

stated before, it is unlikely that more than a hundred or so tons per annum were raised on the Estate in total during the latter half of the 18th century and first half of the 19th century, so Gwaynllifion and Gamfa Fawr cannot have been prolific sources of material.

Not the least problem on these uplands was with water - the lack of it to work machinery or to use in ore dressing processes - and too much of it accumulating in the open workings. It was not uncommon for the miners in these simple 'diggings' to spend more time unwatering the mine than working on the lode. They would be obliged to break all the ore by hand, before carrying it away. On the Gamfa Fawr site the supposed trunk buddle may well have used water carried by bucket from nearby flooded open stopes.

In the event the first occasion on which we have found Gwaynllifion given its name is in those Timber Accounts which have survived for the years 1819 to 1821, when, in the last of them, Owen Owen and Robert Owen were purchasing on behalf of this venture.

No other records relating to individual mines have come to hand for the years prior to 1826, but examination of the Trefriw Port Book does confirm that over sixty vessels carrying lead ore sailed from the Quay between July, 1817 and August, 1826. Not all tonnages were recorded, but it would seem a fair estimate that an average of around 125 tons per annum were shipped. In the Gwydyr context this probably represented eight or ten bargains actually weighing ore, though others may have been let which were not producing ore.

However, the weighing figures for the ten years after 1826 have been preserved, and neither Gwaynllifion nor Gamfa Fawr receive any mention before 1831. In that year two take notes for the former were being exploited, one by Ellis Evans and the other by Owen Jones. Evans had three men at work, but they only stuck it for a couple of years, raising a little over six tons of ore during that period. Jones, on the other hand, with three or four men, raised around fifty tons of ore before a poor year in 1835, and on more than one occasion he brought more ore to market than any of the other eight or ten ventures in Gwydyr that were weighing ore during those years.

After a gap of two years in 1836 and 1837, detailed weighing figures do become available from 1838 onwards, but it was not until 1841 that the Gwaynllifion Nos. 1 and 2 setts were listed, with a No.3 added in 1842. This last venture was only worked on odd occasions until disappearing from the list in 1850. Nothing at all is found for Gamfa Fawr until 1855, about ten years before it emerges as a point of activity in the Gwydyr Park Consols programme for their enlarged Gwaynllifion sett, of which, by that time, it had clearly become a part.

On the evidence of inspection Gamfa Fawr is clearly one of the 'ancient' workings on the Gwydyr Estate, and the absence of reference to it in such records as have survived for the first half of the 19th century add to the belief that it has some antiquity. The workings are on the outcrop of the so-called Red lode, which is almost certainly the Gors lode as it passes in a southerly direction from the Gwydyr Park mine. Figure 4. is a survey of the Gamfa Fawr workings made in 1985.

If we look ahead briefly we will see that Gamfa Fawr attracted a little attention during the early 1860s, at which time a short-lived effort was made to sink on the vein to reach the Gwaynllifion Deep Adit (which will be described below). However, the very minor amount of work described during the 1850s, which was mostly given to clearing old works and washing old hillocks, adds to the impression that the great part of the fairly substantial workings were effected before the end of the 18th century. A detailed survey of this sett may yet indicate that it was worked during the first period of mining activity in Gwydyr during the 17th century, though this can only remain as conjecture at this time.

Prior to 1841 the High Plateau workings were evidently worked in somewhat inconsistent fashion, but for the few years before Gwydyr Park Consols drew them together during the early 1850s, the Gwaynllifion setts at least were worked regularly, albeit without the employment of large numbers of men.

The No.1 sett passed through several hands between 1841 and 1853, and during most of that time the proprietors of the day could claim to be raising and washing good ore, though the twelve tons weighed in 1850 may have been the best year. The No.2 sett had a similar history, and their ore received even more glowing description than that being raised by their immediate neighbour.

One feature of this second Gwaynllifion bargain was that between 1841 and 1851 it was always in the hands of one or another member of the Owen

Fig. 5

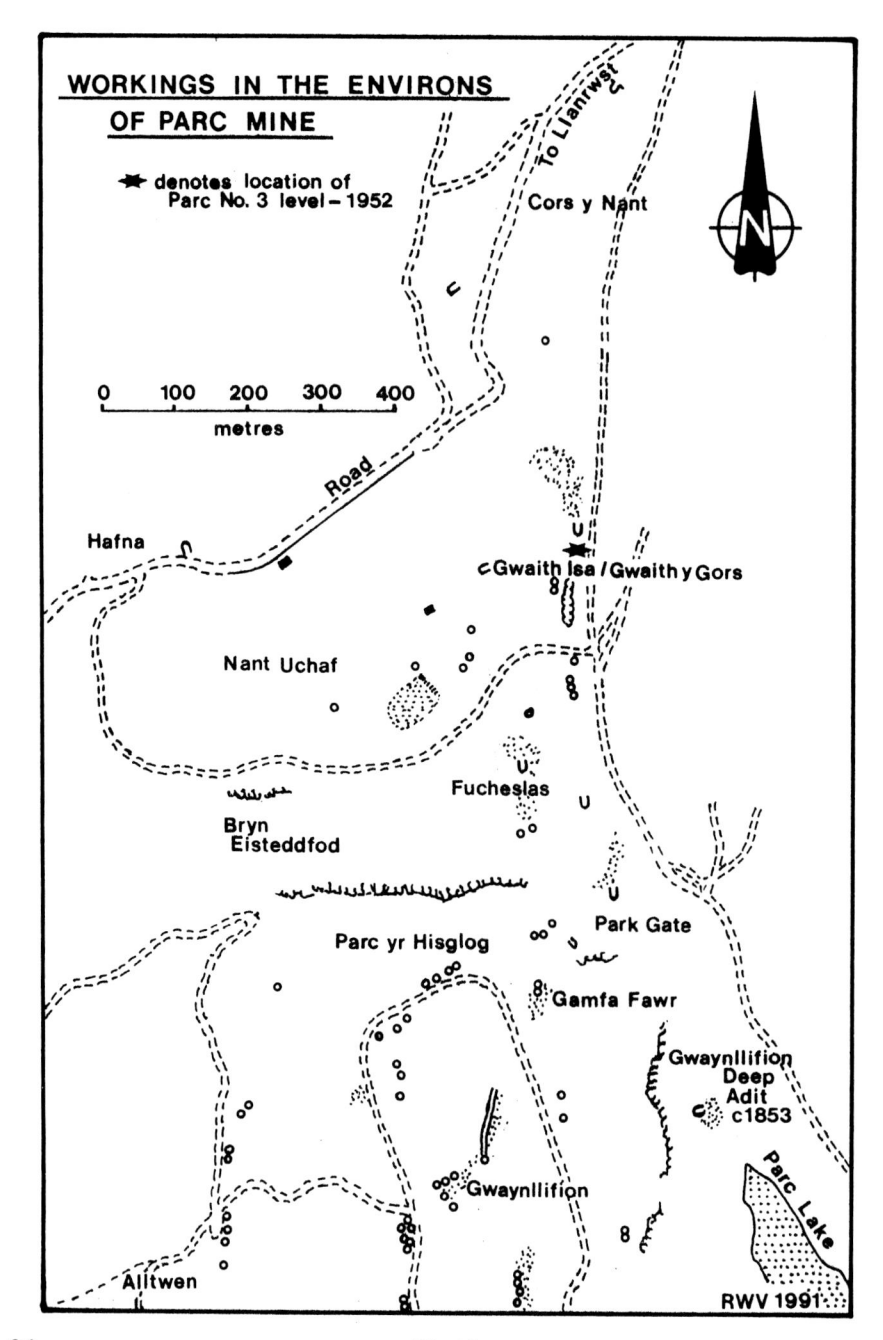

family, either John, Owen or David, and the No.1 sett was also leased to John between 1843 and 1846. Indeed, during the twenty or thirty years after 1838, when the detailed records may be examined, we find either John Owen or Owen Owen involved in approaching twenty different ventures at one time or another in the Betws-y-Coed parish alone, plus a handful in Trewydyr.

It does not come as a surprise, then, that we find Gwydyr Park Consols and their successors sinking Owen's shaft and driving on Owen's lode on their Gwaynllifion property.

The other principal point of work which occupied Gwydyr Consols from the very outset of their involvement in the Gwydyr Estate was the future Gwydyr Park mine, which is the next part of the area which we will discuss. The main pre-Gwydyr Consols ventures in both the Gwaynllifion and Gwydyr areas are shown in Figure 5, where they are described as 'Workings in the environs of Parc mine'.

GWYDYR PARK MINE
PRE-GWYDYR PARK CONSOLS

The feature on this sett which attracted most attention during the 19th century and before, is what came to be known during the 1870s as 'the mighty Gors lode', which courses N-S through the Gwydyr Park ground before entering the Gwaynllifion sett.

In the years prior to 1878 we find no mention of a Gors lode in the records, when the name used for this vein was the Shale lode. This is a little misleading, as the most significant shale lode in the area is found in a major fault which lies to the east of Shale/Gors lode. There are only very minor workings on this major shale lode in the Gwydyr Consols sett, though it was exploited in the Aberllyn sett to the south of Gwydyr. On the other hand the Shale/Gors lode was driven on at an early date and on a series of levels including the Cors y Nant and Gwaith Isa ventures. These will be described below, and the relative success which was met with by the early workers on this lode led to a belief that in Gwydyr the best lead was always found beneath a cap of shale.

In 1878 the then proprietors described two levels driven on this lode to the south of Gwaith Isa, the lower of which was to become significant in later years when Messrs. Brunner Mond drove on it to reach the Principal lode. The upper of these two levels is believed to be the working recorded in the Monthly Returns as Park Gate between 1838 and 1841. At that time only sparks of ore were found, though some shale, or 'black earth', was raised. Between 1855 and 1862 what appears to be the same venture is listed severally as Park or Parc yr Hisglog, when the proprietors were driving the Black Earth vein towards the High Park - or High Plateau.

The first identifiable bargain worked in the Gwydyr Park section of the old Shale/Gors lode, was the Gwaith Isa, which is yet another of the ventures first named in the records when Peter Goodwin, the local mining entrepreneur, was made bankrupt in 1806. On that occasion Gwaith Isa, in which Goodwin held eight ounces, or a half share, was described as 'in full work, and producing a fair quantity of ore'.

Nothing more is known of the venture until the weighing records for the years 1826 to 1835, when the sett was only receiving intermittent attention, and during which years some fifteen to twenty tons of lead ore were weighed. Nor was there any activity at the start of the next period for which detailed records survive, from 1838 onwards.

The next year, 1839, saw the lease in the hands of Messrs. Gregory & Co., who put a couple of men in the mine for a little over a year. They appear to have been searching for the lode, and found spots of lead and zinc ores. However, it may not have been lead or zinc which interested the proprietors, as they also held the lease for Aberllyn on which they were working the authentic Shale lode, where any minor amounts of lead and zinc ores raised may have been incidental to the larger tonnage of 'black earth', or black shale, which they weighed.

When Gregory & Co. left the lease was taken by one John Williams, who worked the Gwaith Isa steadily for the remaining eleven years during which existed under this name. Williams seldom employed more than one or two men, who spent most of their time driving in the level or on cross-cuts, only finding ore worth speaking of on rare occasions.

The Monthly Returns mark the arrival of Gwydyr Park Consols in Gwaith Isa in July of 1853, and in September of that year record the fact that 'Mr. Dean and ten men are now entered on working Gwaith y Gors'. Dean, about whom more later, was directing the efforts of the local management, and Gwaith y Gors is almost certainly a new working on the old Gwaith Isa sett, concentrating effort on a new vein, but with the adit at the same point, or very adjacent to that of Gwaith Isa. This was in the region of what later became known as Kneebone's Cutting.

Another important element in the Gwydyr Park Consols was to be the inclusion, in 1868, of the Fucheslas setts, which lie in the ground between Gwydyr Park mine and Gwaynllifion, where the land falls from the High Plateau towards the Nant Isaf. The situation of Fucheslas, as well as early ventures in the Gwydyr and Gwaynllifion setts, can also be identified in Figure 5.

FUCHESLAS PRE-1868

Fucheslas was very much one of the mountain sides which Watson described as 'riddled with old shafts and scored in all directions with the adits and open cuttings of the old miners', as mentioned above. Certainly there was more than one 'Fycheslas' bargain in the old days, and probably several others ventures in the area whose names have been lost in the mists of time.

The first documented evidence of working on the Fucheslas setts came with a take note, dated 1.1.1819, which has survived in the Plas yn Cefn MSS. Edward Lloyd, whose spread of interest in lead mining in North Wales was touched upon in the previous volume in this series, took up the lease on that date in partnership with three of the local mining family of Harker.

Lloyd had also contracted for a take note for the Glyn sett in 1819, to which he added Hafna in 1821 and Cors y Nant in 1823, but when records become available for 1826 and subsequently, we discover from them that, although he had held onto or renewed his interests in Cors y Nant and Hafna, he had, by that time, relinquished Fucheslas and Glyn.

These last two setts had now become the interest of Robert Hughes & Co., who had received mention in the Timber Accounts for 1820, when he had purchased for Bryn Cenhadon in the adjoining Gwydyr parish of Llanrhychwyn as well as for the Nant sett. In this last venture there appears to have been a good deal of chopping and changing of proprietorship during this period.

Robert Hughes was a Bangor man, who played a substantial part in whatever mining and quarrying took place in Gwydyr during the late 1820s and early 1830s, the latter, in particular, being a period of very restricted activity due to poor economic circumstances in trade. Up to 1830, Hughes generally had four or five men at each of his bargains, and one or the other sett was usually the largest annual producer on the Estate.

However, when things got tougher during the early 1830s he left the Glyn sett to new proprietors and reduced his manpower at Fucheslas to a couple of men. He had been able to weigh some eighty tons of ore from Fucheslas between 1826 and 1830, and a further twenty-three tons between 1831 and 1835, which was quite a determined effort in the context of the Gwydyr Estate. The number of bargains weighing ore in Gwydyr fell to seven during the early 1830s, with well below fifty tons per annum produced, no doubt reflecting the serious depression which was being felt in the industry throughout the country at that time.

Detailed records are again available from 1838, when we find Hughes & Co. still in possession of both the Fucheslas bargains, though they left in 1839 after a period of indifferent success. However, when the two setts were again let in 1842, both of them to David Evans, they entered a phase of relative prosperity, with as many as eight men on each sett at times, and able to raise and wash 'good' or 'very good' ore consistently throughout the period. The quality of the ore remained good after Evans had departed, until the ventures were left a couple of years before Gwydyr Park Consols came on the scene in 1852 - indeed, the ore on the No.2 bargain in 1846 was described by the Agent as 'the strongest ore in view on the Estate'.

There were a good number of adits on the Fucheslas setts, and who worked which and when remains something of a mystery. What is clear is that the most important workings were driven on the Fucheslas lode well below the rising land of the Craig Fucheslas. There were two principal levels at the base of the hill, the deep level and the shallow level, and it seems certain that the extensive and evidently worthwhile workings on Owen's lode in the adjacent Gwaynllifion sett were, in fact, on the southerly extension of the Fucheslas lode.

Before passing on to the Tyn Twll sett this would be an appropriate point to describe the Cors y Nant bargain, as, although this never became a part of Gwydyr Consols, it is much more closely associated with the Gwydyr Park mine and its lodes than is Tyn Twll. As mentioned above, it was another of the works driven (in part) on the wrongly named Shale lode - later better named as the Gors lode - and it was incorporated in the old Gwydyr Park mine sett soon after it passed to the next proprietors, the D'Eresby Mountain Mining Company.

CORS Y NANT

There is at least circumstantial evidence that Cors y Nant may have been one of the principal ventures in Gwydyr during the second half of the 18th century, and before studying such detail as has come to hand, it is interesting to read a description given to it in 1879, when it had been added to the D'Eresby Mountain sett. The lease was purchased in 1878 by the D'Eresby Mountain Company when they had discovered rich ore in the D'Eresby Mountain mine No.4 level some five hundred yards further up the Nant, and on the same lode that Cors y Nant level had been driven. The Cors y Nant level, now described as D'Eresby No.5, was much ruined, but was to be cleared and brought up beneath the lead in the No.4 level to facilitate mining and drainage.

It was after D'Eresby had explored and begun to clear the No.5 that evidence was found to suggest some extensive workings of an early date. In a descriptive article for the Mining Journal in 1879 the proprietors wrote:-

> *When the great Gorse (sic) lode was found in No.4 the grand speculation, as we have always stated, was to see the lode at the deeper level, No.5. The story of the old men who had heard it from others that had worked in it was, that while raising large quantities of lead - 100 tons per month - from No.5, and even below it, for which they had actually erected a waterwheel underground, the level fell in (a thing very probable with a lode of such great width), crushed their waterwheel and timber supports, and stopped all their works.*

Later in the same article a further evidence of antiquity was described:
Among the debris found on Saturday was one of the greatest curiosities we have seen for a long time - an iron borer 12ins. long, embedded in 8ins. of solid lead. It is much corroded, and has, probably, been lying in the debris for upwards of a century.

If this is evidence that a level approaching three hundred fathoms in length existed during the 1770s, complete with underground waterwheel and producing one hundred tons of lead ore per month, then this must have been one of the most significant venture in Gwydyr Nant during the 18th century. In fact, the level may well have been in the region of two hundred fathoms, though the weighing figures offered are well over the top. This was very possibly the venture of Messrs. Ellis & Lloyd and their partners, who were active in the 'Mines in the Nants' for much of the second half of the 18th century. Unfortunately, however, nothing is found in the records to make this suggestion any more than an educated guess.

The earliest specific reference to the bargain which has survived is a mention in the 1820 accounts, when James Harker & Co. were purchasing timber for the mine, and again in 1821, when Harker was purchasing timber 'for Edward Lloyd's mine'. It can be deduced from the Plas yn Cefn Manuscripts that Edward Lloyd of Cefn, who has already been mentioned above in connection with his interest in Fucheslas, purchased the last two years of a take note for Cors y Nant, issued in 1819, from the Harkers, with whom he was already in partnership at Fucheslas. He gave them £50 for the two unexpired years, and when this finished he took out a second take note for the bargain, which was dated 1.1.1823. He was obliged by this second contract to keep four men at work on the sett, which by Gwydyr standards made it a relatively important work.

This lease expired after four years, on 1.1.1827, but Lloyd & Co. remained as proprietors for a further four years after 1827, being followed in 1831 by the Harkers for yet another stint. Lloyd & Co. weighed some thirty-five tons of lead ore between April, 1826 and the end of 1830, as well as around thirty tons from Hafna, though in the five years for which we have details he only managed to employ the required four men in one year.

The Harkers came back to the sett at a time of depression, weighing less than ten tons of ore between 1831 and 1835, nothing at all in 1833, when the economy was at its worst, and never employed more than two or three men in the bargain. They hung on, with little success, until 1841, and Christopher Harker came back for a few weeks with two men in 1847, but aside from that nothing was to happen here until Gwydyr Park Consols had come and gone on the adjoining setts, and D'Eresby Mountain acquired the ground to drive their deep level in 1878.

The last of the pre-Gwydyr Consols points of work, which was to be incorporated in the second Gwydyr Consols Company lease, was the Tyn Twll sett, which is described below.

TYN TWLL PRE-1872

Tyn Twll is one of a series of tenements which lie to the west of the Betws-y-Coed to Conway road below the junction of this road with that from Llanrwst, between Gwydyr Uchaf and Pant y Carw. It should be remembered that Tyn Twll Mine, with which we will be principally concerning ourselves, was formed from the combination of a number of smaller bargains. During the 1830s and 1840s several were named, including Tyn Twll Nos. 1 & 2, Tyn Twll & Rhydloew, Rhydloew Nos. 1 & 2 and Llety. The lease for Tyn Twll Mine in 1853 was described as not only being a part of Tyn Twll, but also parts of Ty'r Mawn and of Ffrithshaune, and in addition to that a bargain on the adjoining Park Stalwyn was added to the Tyn Twll ground in the 1860s.

Tyn Twll has the distinction of being one of the few bargains actually mentioned by name at the time of Dr. Linden's interest in the Estate during the 1750s and 1760s, and it does seem certain that this working would have been on Tyn Twll tenement itself. In fact, later evidence suggests that it may have been very near to the Conway road, where an old shaft and flooded workings are believed to be the earliest to have been tried.

Linden refers to Tyn Twll in two letters which he wrote to a Mr. Williams at Gwydyr in 1763. In the first of these, dated the 9th of August he wrote:

> '–in regard of Tyn Twll I have informed Mr. Thomas that I am very sure that they may work this bargain without the level, and that His Grace will never be at any such expense, and therefore as soon as any such level becomes necessary it must be set to Adventurers, to be at that expense, but in the meantime to work in a good condition, and rise as much ore upon the time as possible.'

Lord Ancaster had been a loser in the Trefrew Company, which had been trying for ore on the Estate during 1753 and 1754, probably investing on the advice of his mining consultant, Linden, who was therefore most anxious that his employer should not catch another financial cold in the Tyn Twll venture

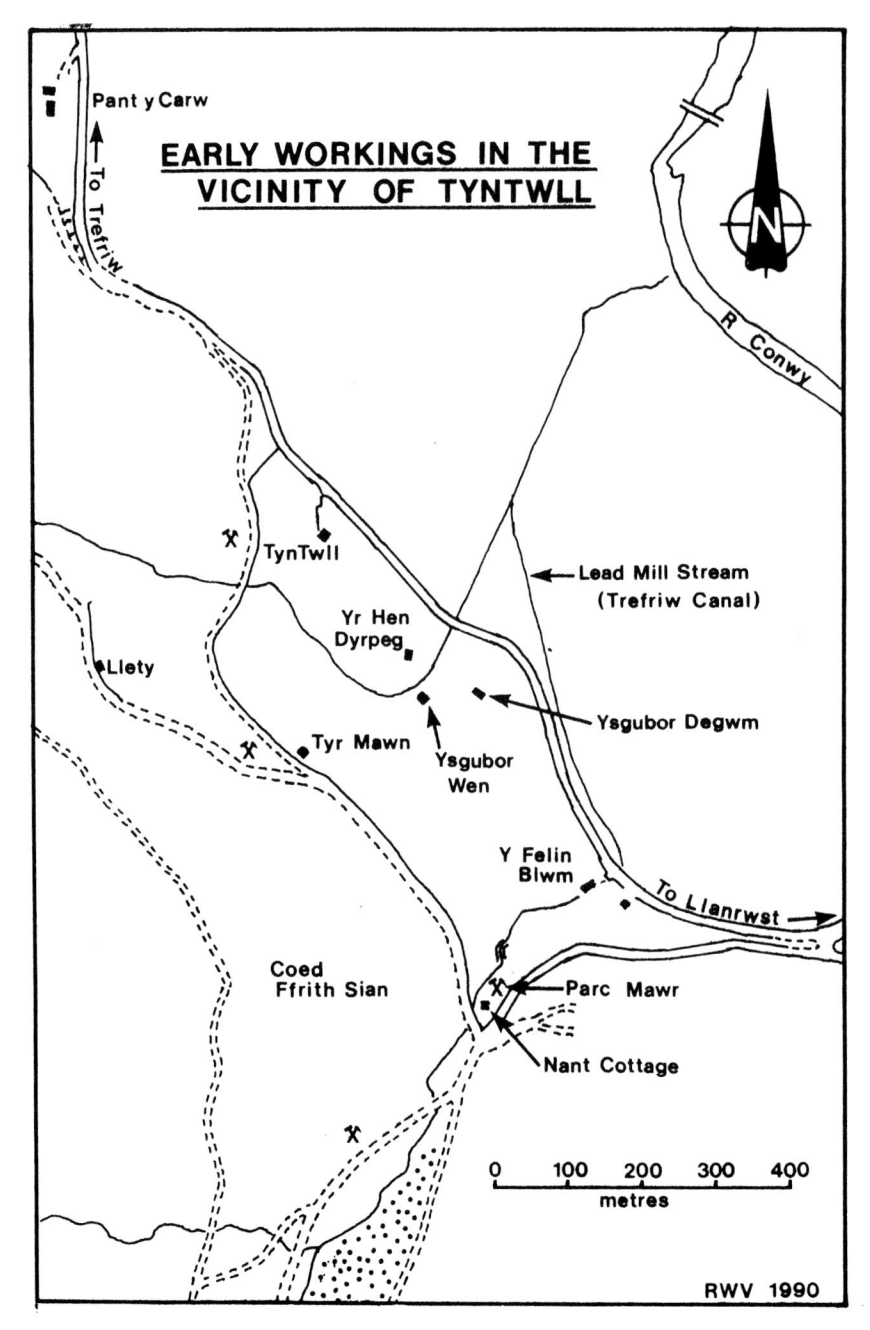

Fig. 6

- hence his unwillingness to recommend any substantial development work. Linden re-emphasised this point in a second letter dated 27th of August, when he warned against any extravagant demands, and repeated that *'His Grace would not be at any expense - and therefore you must not meddle with it in that way'*. The evidence seems to be that from the early 1750s onwards, probably for the best part of a hundred years, the proprietors were prepared to put their own men to work on occasional ventures, probably paying them a wage rather than leasing them a bargain and taking royalties. They were not willing, however, to spend any sum in the development of the mines.

The tenement of Parc Ysgubor Wen, which adjoined Tyn Twll to the south, was also an area steeped in the early history of Gwydyr mining, as it was here, according to local historians, that the old roads from Gwydyr Nant and from Llanrhychwyn made their way down to the main road in the Conway valley. When the miners carrying ore from the mountain reached this point they found themselves paying a toll at Yr Hen Dyrpeg before they could carry on to the quay at Trefriw, from where they shipped their ore onwards to the smelters. Tradition states that they then cut a new road, which is still seen on the map passing between Ty'r Mawn and Pant y Carw on the main road. This road passes over a ford, or rhyd, on the Tyn Twll boundary, and it is very tempting to believe that this is the rhyd of Rhydloew found in the leases of the 1840s. When the tollgate was moved to its present position near the Pant y Carw quarry yet another road was cut to avoid it, descending the steep road down Allt yr Ysfa direct to the village of Trefriw.

To the west of the Parc Ysgubor Wen, at the side of the Llanrhychwyn road, lies Llety, or 'the Inn'. After a break of many years this building is now once more a 'lodging place', and is proud to recall its ancient history.

South of Parc Ysgubor Wen lies the Parc Mawr, site of another bargain which saw activity at a very early stage in the development of Gwydyr. Linden had been obliged to bring miners from other parts of Wales to the Estate, as there was a dearth of experience locally, and in John William's accounts for the year of 1755 we learn of 'the Cardiganshire miners and labourers' being paid on account of their bargains at both Park Mawr and 'Bwlch Heirn'.

Another interesting feature on Park Mawr is 'Felin Blwm', or the 'Lead Mill'. This may or may not have been the Lead Mill in Trefriw which is listed as paying rent during the 1750s, and it may or may not have milled much lead - evidence has not been forthcoming on this point. However, it was a focal point for yet another attempt to get Gwydyr Nant lead ore to Trefriw at the least possible cost.

This was to be by canal from the Felin Blwm, utilising the waters of the Nant Gwyd, which below the Felin Blwm came to be known as Lead Mill Stream. When this project was first embarked upon is not clear, though Hyde Hall, in his 'Description of Carnarvonshire, 1809-11', speaks of a canal to the Conway 'which had once been begun'. The idea was still attracting attention as late as 1820, as the Estate records for that year list expenses when two men were contracted to cut the old canal '- 7ft. wide at the top, 4ft. wide at the bottom and 3ft. deep, for 1s. each eight yards'. This turned out to be a very short-lived effort, and the work was left incomplete.

Between 1817 and 1823 the leasing and supervision of the mines, and the weighing of ore became the responsibility of Evan Pritchard, who became interested in mining on his own account, and he took a take note to work a mine on Park Mawr in 1819. There is no evidence that he met with any success in this venture, but he did take an increasing hand in mining matters in general in the area, and in 1825 he replaced John Hooson & Co as the purchaser of the Gwydyr Estate ore. This comprised in part of ore raised directly by men employed by the Estate, but in greater quantity the 'farm' ore, or royalty, paid by lessees on the numerous bargains.

It appears that there was something of a lull in activity in the 'Tyn Twll Group' during the 1820s and 1830s, and there well may have been for some years before this, as later commentators suggest that Tyn Twll was left when it became inundated with water at an early stage of its development. Whether this was so or not, there was certainly no mention of these bargains either in the Timber Accounts for 1819 to 1821, or in the Weighing Book for 1826 to 1835, and the first reference to be found in the Monthly Returns available from 1838 describes them in that year as being leased to Messrs. W. & R. Owen, but standing due to water.

Between 1841, when an effort was begun to open up the old workings, and the advent of Hugh Hughes on the sett in 1853, it appears that there was some rationalisation of the many minor bargains, and attention was paid to sinking a new shaft some distance up the hill to the west of Tyn Twll. This became the point of work of a series of small partnerships, who were finding good ore through the late 1840s, though seldom employing more than two or three men, and only weighing seven or eight tons of lead ore a year at best.

This changed with the arrival of a new proprietor, Hugh Hughes, who was initially described as being of Liverpool, but who appears to have taken residence on the Tyn Twll property early during his tenure of the mine. He very soon increased employment to over twenty men, as well as installing a waterwheel, which greatly improved the possibilities for draining and working the prospect. This enabled him to return to the original and evidently productive roadside workings, which had been given up many years before due to flooding, and in 1857 he was able to weigh the heady total of ninety-six tons of lead ore.

Sadly, the machinery broke in 1858, flooding the lower part of the mine, after which things never got back quite to where they had been before that event, though that year and the next put together did see over one hundred tons of ore weighed. Hughes tried a water balance to solve his problems, though perhaps with mixed success, as the records suggest that Hughes rethought his approach to the mine after this disaster, concentrating more effort on the workings higher up the hill. Nothing much was to come from the new approach, however, as he had evidently died by early 1860, when the lease passed to his widow, Sarah Hughes.

From that point on nothing much seems to have been done at Tyn Twll beyond dealing with lead ore which was ready in the mine or had previously been brought to grass. The mine was at a stand by July of 1862, except for a couple of men washing the old hillocks, and the waterwheel, iron rails and all the machinery except the water balance had been sold in June to T. Swift, Esq., of Tyn y Bryn quarry. This quarry lay a few miles away in Dyffryn Lledr, and Swift proposed to use the waterwheel on this site, but to sell the remainder of the machinery.

The mine was at a stand from 1862 until Robert Williams came to work on tribute for Sarah Hughes in 1869, purportedly making himself £160 profit for a few months work, raising and washing over forty tons of lead ore. The transfer of the lease to Jehu Hitchens & Co. in November of 1872 marked the arrival of the second of the two Gwydyr Consols Companies mentioned above.

GWYDYR PARK CONSOLS (Cost Book) 1853 - 1870

The late 1840s and early 1850s were significant years for the Gwydyr mines, as it was then that they first began to attract the attention of promoters and mining stock and share brokers in London and other important commercial centres. In the event, the lease for Gwaynllifion and Gwydyr Consols Lead Mines (i.e. Gwaynllifion and Gwaith Isa, or Gwaith y Gors setts), which formed the original basis of the Gwydyr Park Consols, was obtained by Nicholas Harvey of Hale Foundry in Cornwall and Richard Tredinnick of Gresham House, Old Broad Street, London, who was one of the Tredinnick family who were in business as Stock and Sharebrokers at that time, with Offices in both London and Hayle.

The lease secured their rights from the 2nd of May, 1853, for a period of twenty-one years, with a royalty to be paid of one tenth of the ore produced, and requiring an undertaking from them to keep ten men employed in the mines. Rather unusually for Gwydyr lessees they comfortably kept up their obligations in this last commitment through the seventeen years that this company existed, indeed, in many years the total workforce on the two setts comfortably exceeded the ten men promised.

The first work on the ground occurred in the Gwaynllifion sett in 1852, when, according to the Monthly Returns, Arthur Dean put eleven men to opening and driving in both the shallow and adit levels and to building a smithy. In the other mine Dean started to clear the old level in Gwaith Isa in July of 1853, and the last entry for this sett was to the effect that 'Mr. Dean and ten men now entered on working Gwaith y Gors'.

Arthur Dean was Consulting Engineer to the Gwydyr Consols Company, and was a man of considerable reputation, whose particular claim to fame was that he was generally credited with having been the first person to recognise the presence of gold in the Merionethshire mines. He put Henry Rawson, a local Mine Captain, in charge of the two ventures, and Rawson was to stay until 1860. In that year he was replaced by William Smyth, who remained in charge until the second Gwydyr Consols company was on its last legs during the early 1870s.

Throughout the period from 1853 to the finish of the Cost Book Company in 1870 the two setts - though sharing management and workforce - worked quite independently, and it is convenient to separate them while looking at their respective progress.

The principal point in the Gwaynllifion venture was to drive a deep level beneath a series of N-S lodes on the Gwydyr High Plateau, some of which had been extensively worked from the surface, with the promise of rich lead below workings which had been left due to inundation by water. To effect this an adit level was driven from the north end of the Parc Lake, a great part of which came to be driven on the ENE-WSW coursing Sutton's lode.

The initial phase of activity saw as many as thirty men at work driving in the deep adit, which had reached twenty-eight fathoms by July of 1854, after two years driving. The shallow adit, which was more productive of ore, had reached forty-four fathoms by the same date. Throughout the years that the Gwaynllifion deep adit was receiving attention it always proved to be a much more expensive undertaking as regards driving than the Gwydyr deep adit, ranging up to £14 per fathom on occasion - almost twice the Gwydyr costs. This was only partially offset by ore production in the Gwaynllifion mine, and to effect this it was necessary, even then, to take the men out of the deep adit and put them into the shallow adit, which was not thought to be the best way of employing them in the long run.

This may have been the reason that the management rather neglected Gwaynlifion during the late 1850s and early 1860s. However, they maintained a steady effort in the deep adit between 1863 and 1867, usually employing seven to ten men in the adit or in sinking a shaft to reach this adit at about one hundred fathoms from the portal.

As mentioned above, the deep adit was driven generally in an E-W direction, though for some distance ENE-WSW on what came to be known as Sutton's lode - taking this name from a prominent Director of the Company. The plan of the deep adit in Figure 10 was actually surveyed in the 1950s, when some differences were made in the interpretation of the lodes. However, it is included at this juncture, as almost the entire drivage and workings on the lodes had been completed by 1878.

A lot of thought had been given by Arthur Dean as to where it might be advantageous to sink an engine shaft to this adit, but it eventually took over twenty-five years before a suitable spot was chosen - many years after Dean had gone. In reaching this spot the deep level had been driven some two hundred fathoms, and cut some eight N-S lodes, the significant ones being the Red lode and Owen's lode (which were later to be described as the Gors lode and the Fucheslas lode in the Gwydyr sett to the north), and the New lode.

An abortive attempt was made to sink what was described as Newton's shaft on the Red lode in 1863, in the old Gamfa Fawr workings. Six men were contracted to sink this shaft at £5 per fathom, and it was anticipated that they would reach a short drive north on the Red lode from the deep adit in seven to eight months. However, they were quickly stopped by water and the scheme abandoned.

An old shaft on Owen's lode was considered for the engine, but in the end it was decided to sink a shaft on the intersection of Sutton's lode and the New lode. This shaft was eventually to communicate with the deep adit in 1870, and it was here that the 'fire engine' was placed in the same year. This shaft had previously been known as Rawson's shaft, though Rawson had left the mine long before it reached its objective in the deep adit - it was later to become known as Sutton's shaft. From this point it was proposed to continue the drive west on Sutton's lode, which was expected to get under another of the significant N-S lodes. This was the Cobbler's lode, from which a family of local shoemakers were held to have made a considerable fortune in earlier days, allowing them to build several houses in the neighbourhood.

The importance of the connection between the adit and the shaft will be discussed below, after the Gwydyr Consols mine has been described, as, with the deep adit in Gwydyr, it was one of the two significant achievements which gave impetus to the formation of the second Gwydyr Consols Company in 1870.

The Gwydyr Consols Mine compares with its partner at Gwaynllifion in that the principal effort over all the seventeen years of the first Consols Company was to carry a deep adit under purportedly rich old workings, though Gwydyr was a more extensive and developed prospect. The clue to its relationship to the older workings comes from the special general meeting of shareholders in 1857, which stated that the Gwydyr mine adit had been commenced from the glen by former workers driving N-S to the Gwaith Isa shaft thereon. (i.e. the Gwydyr deep adit, or future D'Eresby No.4 level driven to what developed into Kneebone's Cutting in the 1890s.)

The report to the shareholders continued by explaining that the present Company were driving west from the Gwaith Isa shaft towards the Fucheslas lode, on what they knew as the Cross Mawr level. This working was evidently known as Gwaith y Gors to distinguish it from Gwaith Isa. They proposed coming under Johnnies shaft and Harker's mine on the Fucheslas lode, which was where they anticipated rich returns.

A good deal of development inside and outside the mine occurred in association with this project, including the laying of a railway and installation of an air machine in the level, and the erection of a crushing machine, store house, etc., on the dressing floor near to the adit. As mentioned above, one advantage of Gwydyr when compared to Gwaynllifion was that the driving costs were generally only about half those pertaining to Gwaynllifion, and they were substantially defrayed by the weighing off and selling of over one hundred tons of lead ore during what was strictly a development phase, whereas Gwaynllifion only raised twenty tons or so of lead ore and blende during the same period.

Throughout its history this Company gave every impression that it was a genuine concern with genuine prospects, and it seems that the shareholders were quite prepared to answer the calls without the proprietors needing to resort to the extravagent rhetoric that accompanied too many ventures in this area. After some ten years of work the Secretary, Jehu Hitchens, commented that expenditure of 17/9d on each of the 6068 shares in issue had been encountered, but income from the sale of ore had only realised £857.3s.0d. This did not dissuade the shareholders from continuing to shell out for calls at much the same rate, and with much the same returns of ore, for a further seven years. Indeed, in 1863, the local Manager, Captain William Smyth, felt able to write that he was 'willing to carry out the small share that I hold now, and am sorry I am not in a position to take more'. On this occasion one might be disposed to believe him. Reports in the Mining Journal in 1870 indicated that by the beginning of that year calls had amounted to £1.14s.d. per share, while business was being done at between £1.0s.0d. and £1.10s.0d. per share - no dividend having been paid during the seventeen years of the venture, though high hopes were still being entertained.

At this juncture the great point of years of endeavour was about to be reached in both mines, with communications to the deep adit levels in Gwaynllifion and Gwydyr about to be effected. Comment in the Watson Brothers Mining Circular, which appeared in the Mining Journal dated the 19th of December, 1868, pointed to the fact that the 'heavy brigade' had arrived in Gwydyr, or were about to do so, and the Watsons, Mineowners, Stock and Share Dealers, took an increasingly central role in the promotion of this group of mines over the ensuing years.

Gwydyr Park Consols seemed to them at that time 'an excellent speculation at a very low price indeed' into which there was 'very little risk in buying'. With the encouragement and advice of these eminent city gentlemen the shareholders of the Cost Book Company persuaded themselves that the next step should be to form a Limited Liability Company. The first move in that direction was for J. Y. Watson to join the committee of management, which was confirmed at a general meeting of shareholders in April of 1870.

> At that meeting the Chairman, Mr. W. S. Sutton, remarked that - *'the important work which had been so long in progress was now nearly completed; and although two years had elapsed since ore had been sold, not by reason of the poverty of the mine, but solely on account of the work now being carried on to effect ventilation, the time was, he hoped, not far distant when from realised results Gwydyr Park would vie with many of the fashionable Welsh lead mines now so favourably regarded by the public.'*

It was further agreed that a special general meeting should be held during the next month, for the purpose of taking the necessary steps for registering the Company, with 12,000 shares, with limited liability.

GWYDYR PARK CONSOLS (Limited Liability), 1870-1874

This Company was incorporated on the 9th of July in 1870 to acquire the Gwaynllifion and Gwydyr Park Consols setts from the Cost Book Company. These extended to some forty-two acres, to which they were soon to add thirty-two acres of the Tyn Twll & Llety sett. The 12,000 shares had a nominal value of 30s. per share of which 25s. was credited as paid. The Chairman, W. S. Sutton, stayed on with his relatively large holding, Jehu Hitchens stayed on as Secretary, and the Watsons became large shareholders in the concern.

To the shareholders who had persevered with the old Company and stayed with the new, the year 1870 must have seemed to be most auspicious. Not only had Gwydyr Consols pursued what they were reassured was the expedient course of reforming itself under limited liability, it had also in the same year effected what were held to be the great points of the work of the old Company by the driving of the two deep adits in Gwaynllifion and Gwydyr to the places under the old workings to which they had aspired, and, also in 1870, they had also communicated the deep levels to the surface, so overcoming the increasing problem of ventilation which they had been encountering. Little did they know then that they would have left both these workings within a year or so, blown the capital - plus additional money called from them - and seen the Company wound up by 1874.

However, back in 1870 the shareholders had been treated to a report from John Roberts, a local Mining Captain in whom a good deal of confidence was placed - and they must have found this reassuring. Roberts had no hesitation - in his own words - in saying that the Gwaynllifion lodes would be rich in depth, and that in the Gwydyr Mine they would find a rich and lasting deposit of lead, equal, as he put it, to the most sanguine expectations.

When the first general meeting was held that year there was a rare shaft of honesty when Robert's report came to be discussed. First of all the Mine Captain, Smyth, declined to make any comment, referring the shareholders to the Company Secretary, Jehu Hitchens, who actually admitted that as yet they had been unable to test the accuracy of the statement that many of the old workings were rich in lead.

These two must have known something, as the next year saw the engine removed from Gwaynllifion and the mine left to a handful of tributers, while Smyth was only allowed to put men in Gwydyr to work in spots where they were guaranteed of immediate results - sometimes known as 'picking the eyes'! However, they were meeting with some success at their new sett at Tyn Twll & Llety - though here again, as so often, the claims for a rosy future were grossly exaggerated.

J. Y. Watson had negotiated the purchase of the Tyn Twll venture on behalf of the Company for the sum of £250, and stated in July of 1871 that he was prepared there and then to buy it back from the Company for £1000. Perhaps Gwydyr Consols missed a bargain at that point, but Watson can never have wholly let go of this property, as he was to make plenty out of it when the Clementina Mining Company took over on this sett at the end of the 1870s.

The earliest, and possibly the richest workings at Tyn Twll appear to have been executed on the E-W lode on which the Roadside shaft had been sunk.

When driven out by water the old men had sunk a shaft some distance west on the hillside, where they had discovered an important N-S lode. This came to be the Engine shaft of Gwydyr Park Consols during their phase of activity, as well as that of the Clementina Mining Company which succeeded them.

When Gwydyr Consols took up the mine this shaft, on which they soon erected the 'fire engine' from Gwaynllifion, was some twenty-three fathoms deep, and one of the first priorities was to sink and secure this shaft to twenty-five fathoms, from which point they were in a position to get some twelve fathoms under supposedly rich ore. Driving was to take place on more than one level on the N-S lode, as well as to some extent on two E-W lodes which were cut - the proprietors still hoping to get under the rich old workings to the east of Engine shaft.

They undoubtably met with some rapid success, as the use of the steam engine enabled them to make a much better hand than their predecessors in this mine, who had been constantly battling with water without the proper means of dealing with it. This appears to be one of the few occasions when a new proprietor could honestly claim that the previous workers had left rich lead ore in the mine when they left!

Between the middle of June in 1871, and March of 1874 there were on average twenty men on the mine - 1873, for instance, saw six men driving and ten men stoping, as well as several at work above ground. They managed to raise and dress almost one hundred and twenty tons of lead ore during this period, though this did not match up to the twenty tons per month which Hitchens had promised them at the outset of the venture.

By the beginning of 1873 there was a new Mine Captain, William Bennetts, and he could evidently see financial trouble looming, as he was very soon suggesting the construction of a reservoir and waterwheel, which would enable them to be less dependent on expensive steam power. He, like so many others in similar situations elsewhere, saw the redemption of the mine as being to sink deeper '- to bring the mine into profitable dividend-paying state'.

Matters had come to a head in January of 1874, when, even though the concern had been able to command over fifteen hundred pounds from ore sales, the cash had run out. An extraordinary general meeting of shareholders during that month was offered the opportunity to put up the money for a further 12,000 Preference Shares at 6s. per share, but when only 315 shares had been subscribed for by March of that year it was necessary to wind the Company up.

This is the point where the various concerns which were the interest of Gwydyr Consols appear to split up and go off in their own directions, as appeared in Figure 3. However, though Tyn Twll, Gwydyr and Gwaynllifion mines all became the interest of new and separate companies by the end of the 1870s, they were very much associated in their proprietorship. The Watson firm of Mineowners, etc., were instrumental in floating the Tyn Twll venture as the Clementina Mining Company in 1876, the Gwydyr Park venture as the D'Eresby Mountain Mining Company in 1877, and the Gwaynllifion venture as the D'Eresby Consols Mining Company in 1878. Along with the Aberllyn Mining Company, which was also floated by the Watsons in 1878, they comprised what came to be known as the D'Eresby Mountain group of mines.

The Watsons chose to describe the Craig Fucheslas and the Gwydyr High Park as the D'Eresby Mountain, one supposes, out of deference to the landlord. During the 1870s this was Clementina, Baroness Willoughby de Eresby, which also accounts for the name of the first of the group to reach the market - the Clementina Mining Company. Prior to this there had been two Willoughby mines in Gwydyr, one so named during the 1850s on the Penrallt sett and a second during the early 1870s on the Pandora sett.

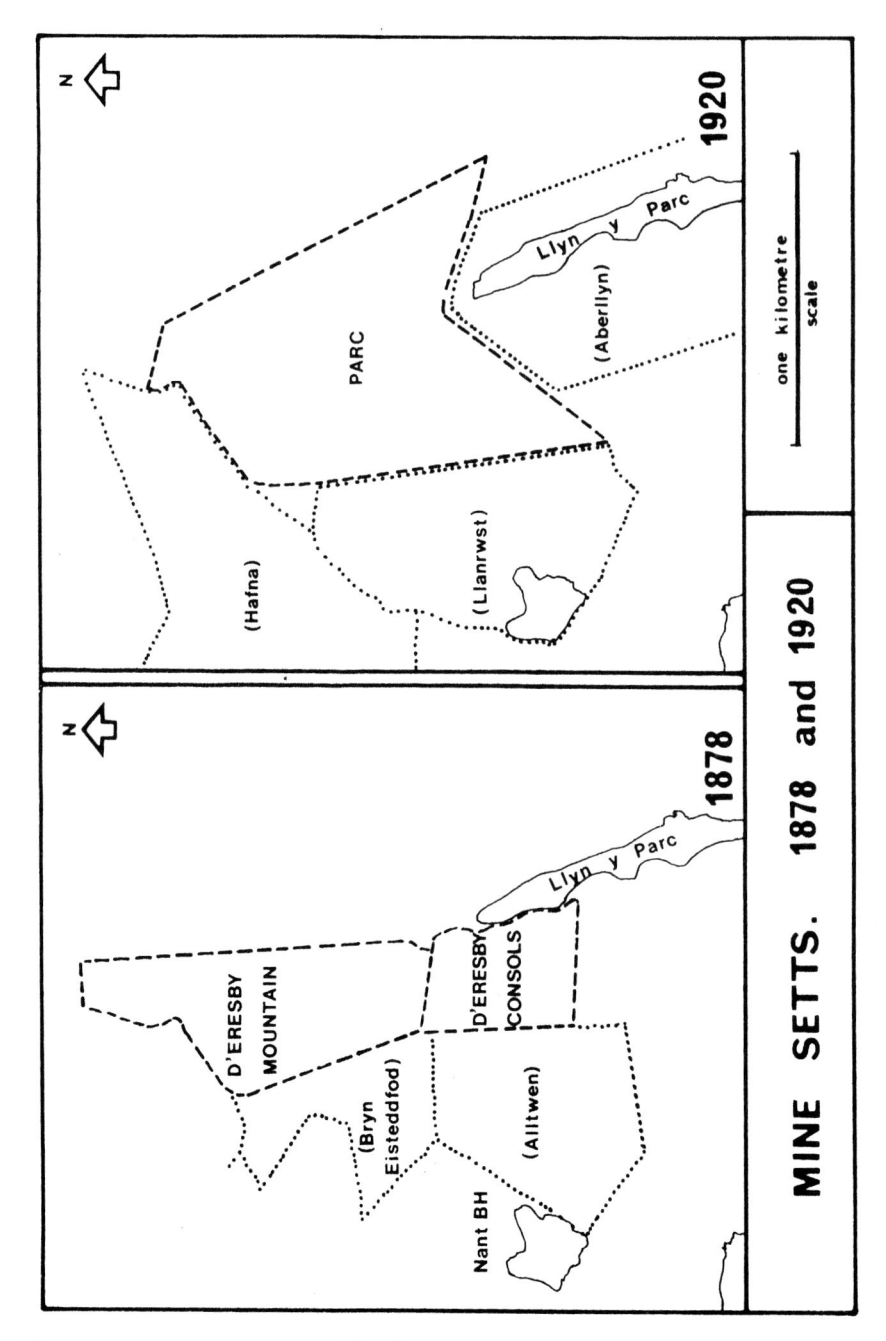

Fig. 7

CLEMENTINA MINING COMPANY 1876 - 1883

When Messrs. Cruikshank and Jehu Hitchens fulfilled their obligations as Liquidators of the Gwydyr Park Consols by disposing of the lease and equipment they evidently did not have to look far for purchasers. When the Clementina Mining Company came to be incorporated two years later we discover that this Company purchased the concern for £550 in cash from Henry Emanuel, who had been a large shareholder in Gwydyr Park Consols. Emanuel was a Subscriber to the Clementina Company, as were Hitchens, ex-Secretary of the Gwydyr Park Consols Company and J. Y. Watson. The new Secretary was C. B. Parry, who was associated with the Watsons in many of their promotions.

The Clementina Mining Company was registered on the 11th of October in 1876, having a share capital of £2560 divided into one hundred and twenty-eight £20 shares. Within the next couple of years these shares were sub-divided into 2560 shares of £1, and a further 2560 shares of £1 issued. Evidently even this was insufficient capital to develop the mine as the proprietors had hoped, and the concern had run out of funds and been wound up by February 1881. It then passed into the hands of a new company, the Gwydyr Amalgamated Mining Company, about which more later.

Clementina appears to have been floated inconspicuously by J. Y. Watson, who gathered a band of supporters after his public denouncement in the Mining Journal of those who had caused damage to the mining interest by forming companies which, as he wrote, '- *had been formed ostensibly for working mines, but in reality to put large sums into the hands of promoters and owners of setts*'.

Having established himself as an honest broker, Watson then went on to describe the mine and its prospects, the gist of which was that if the Engine shaft were sunk a further ten fathoms to a thirty-five fathom level, and if a more effective waterwheel was erected than had previously been the case, then the proprietors would be put in a position to return twenty tons of lead per month, making it possible to pay an annual dividend of £14, or 70% per annum.

John Roberts, who was the Consulting Engineer to this and other mines in Gwydyr, also wrote enthusiastically about the prospects for Clementina and its neighbours - he could even be said to have waxed lyrical, and his

Surface Plan of
CLEMENTINA MINE

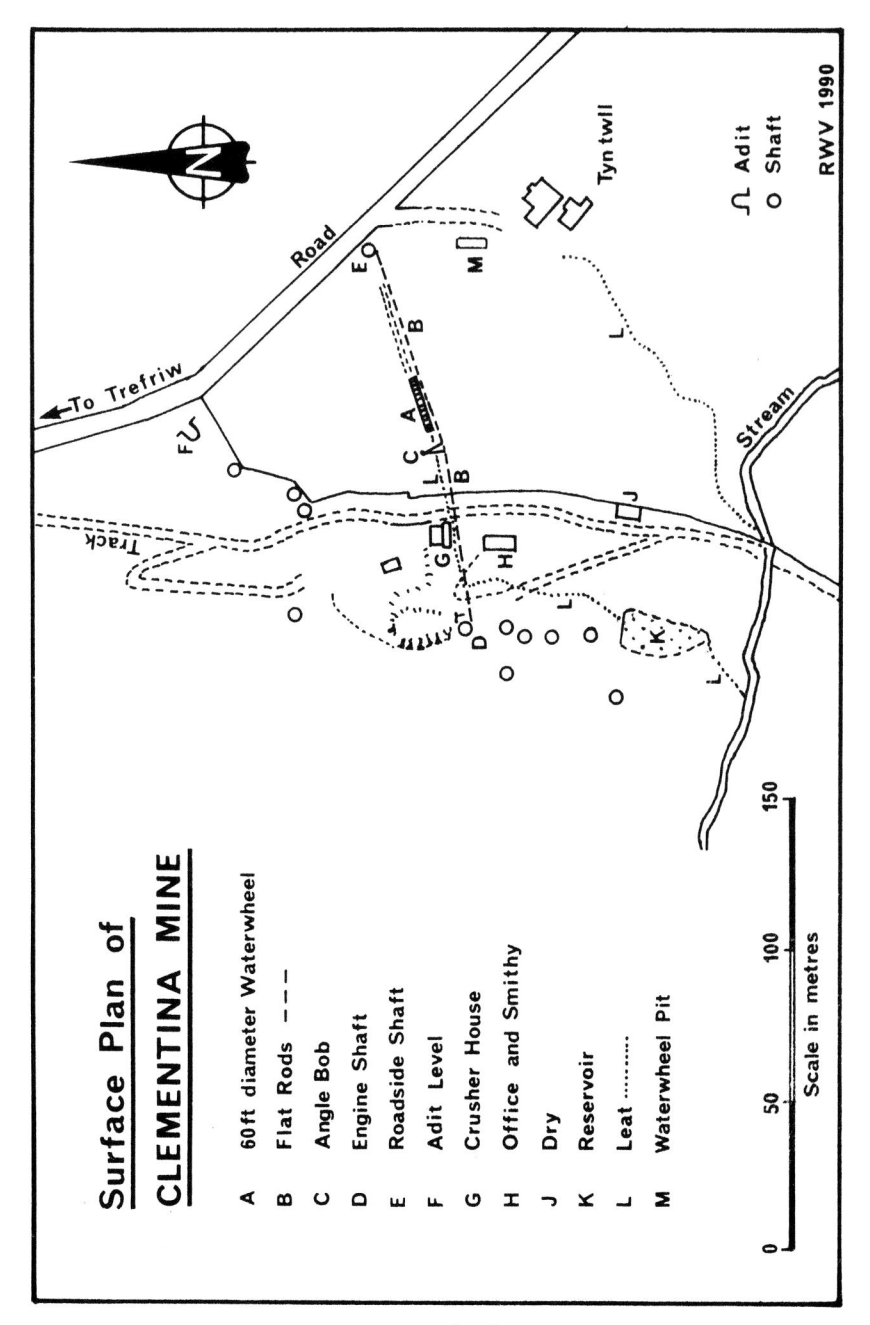

A   60ft diameter Waterwheel
B   Flat Rods - - -
C   Angle Bob
D   Engine Shaft
E   Roadside Shaft
F   Adit Level
G   Crusher House
H   Office and Smithy
J   Dry
K   Reservoir
L   Leat ....
M   Waterwheel Pit

∩ Adit
O Shaft

RWV 1990

Fig. 8

description of the area which appeared in the Mining Journal in June of 1877 even bore comparison with the emanations of Robert Knapp, who managed the nearby Llanrwst Mine during the 1870s, and about whom we have written in the first part of this series.

> Roberts wrote - *'perhaps there is no district which combines more objects of interest than this, and I can scarcely imagine how any man could spend a few days here without feeling fully satisfied that his time had not been spent in vain. Be he a poet, here is something equal to the broadest stretch of his imagination, even in his most gifted hour; be he an artist, the shades and tints, and endless variety of hues delicately painted by the silent hand of the vernal spring, from the valley to the mountain top, and as far distant as the eye can reach, form subjects the most enchanting that his ingenious mind can concieve, or his skillful hand with the richest pigments portray; be he a geologist, he will read on the rocks and reefs where laid bare by the soft beating of the raindrops, or the harder blow of the miner's pick that there lay concealed vast stores of glittering treasure; be he a mineralogist, not only specimens shall he find, but rocks of solid lead that defy his strength to lift them; or be he a capitalist seeking a place to invest his accumulated gold here he will find safe security, only let him be careful that his money finds its way into the mines instead of some promoters pockets.'*

What the speculators actually got for their accumulated gold was a small mine, which was sunk between twenty and thirty fathoms, and in which no levels had been developed beyond a few fathoms, where water in the mine was a chronic problem and lack of water to drive the wheel and machinery was a second chronic problem. The previous company on the sett had gone to the wall trying to make the venture work. However, there was evidently no problem in raising the two tranches of capital, in 1876 and again in 1878, and during the early years of the venture the shares stood at a substantial premium.

John Roberts, Consulting Engineer, and William Sandoe, Mine Captain, set out, with the modest capital which they commanded, to develop the potential both underground and on the surface. The key to this was to be the sixty foot waterwheel, with reservoir to overcome the problems which had previously been experienced on this sett when the stream ran low. This was to be erected in a cavity between the Engine shaft and the Roadside shaft, where the lode had been worked to the surface (or more likely from the surface) by earlier workers - quite possibly back in the days of Dr. Lindens superintendancy during the 1750s and 1760s. This wheel would supply sufficient power to obviate the necessity for an expensive steam engine on the Engine shaft and would enable a return to the workings beneath the Roadside shaft - the positions of both this wheel and its forerunner, that of Hughes, who was active prior to 1862 - are shown in Figure 9. In addition they proposed to extend the capability of the dressing floors, which were only capable of dealing with twenty tons of ore per month.

Everybody seemed quite happy with these plans and predictions, and the development work was put in hand. However, the first instalment of capital did not go very far, after the expenses of purchasing the mine and equipment and setting up the Company had been met, and more capital had to be raised. At the annual meeting in 1878 the management were a bit more cautious, however, when they told the shareholders that the new injection of cash was required, only claiming on this occasion that this would put them in a position to raise ten tons per month - nor was the wheel yet in place.

Even with additional financial support matters proceeded slowly, and the wheel had still not been erected by the 1879 annual meeting, though, happily for all, the Agents were '- still very sanguine of success'. And some success they indubitably had, as the annual meeting of 1880 learnt from them that the Engine shaft had reached thirty-four fathoms, at which depth levels were being driven, that lead ore was being raised and that the waterwheel was working. The Chairman at that meeting, Mr. J. Y. Watson, was able to report that the Agents would show that the mine had prospects second to none in the district. They never had greater confidence in the mine, and it had never looked so good. But the money had run out. The shareholders were offered the usual baits - a final instalment of capital, a few more fathoms sinking, etc., but they had had enough - they had paid wages for between ten and twenty men for over four years, much of the work being done in the mine, and had only seen something just over sixty tons of lead ore raised.

However, there was one more significant piece of business which the Clementina proprietors had executed early in the history of the concern, and it may have been that the shareholders were somewhat mollified by this.

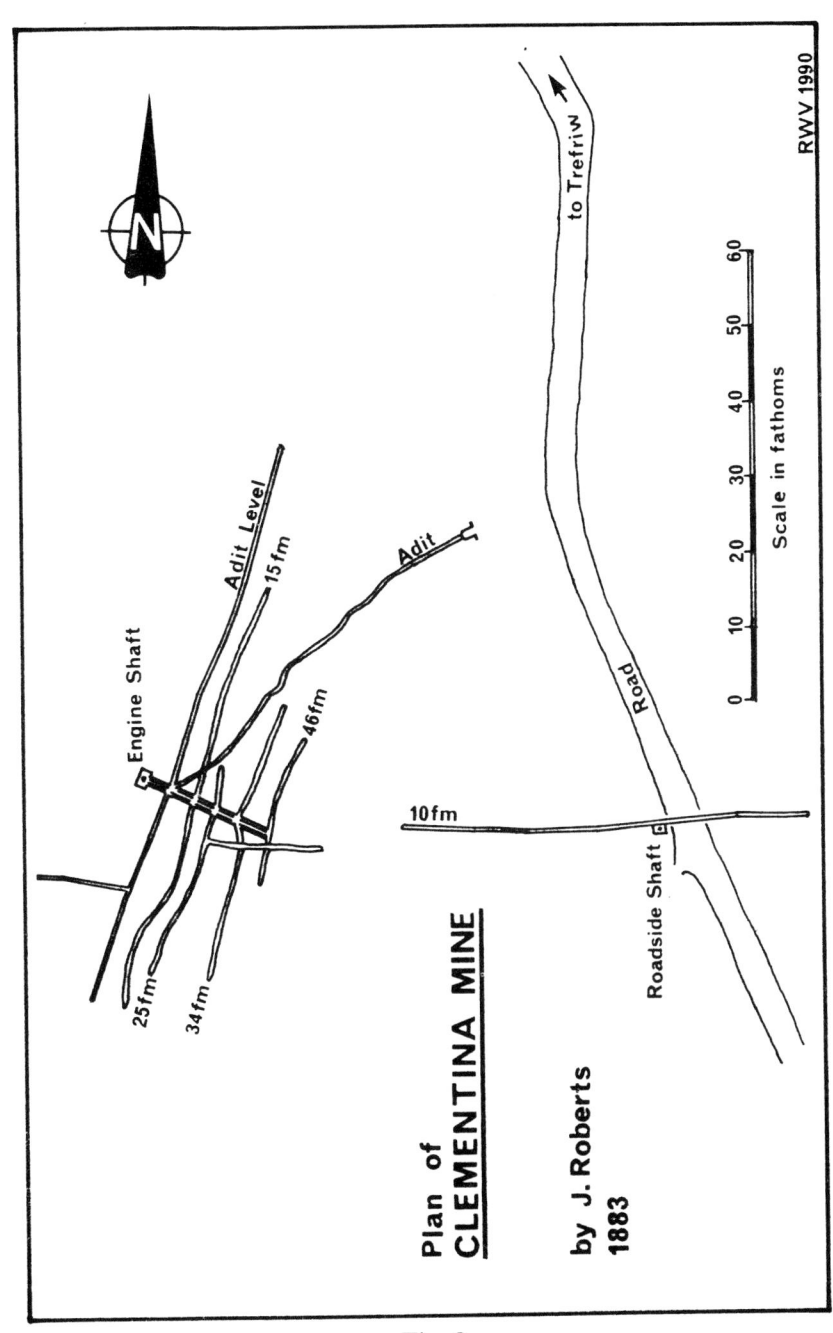

Fig. 9

In 1877 the Company 'discovered' that as well as the lease for the Tyn Twll Mine, it also held the lease for the nearby 'D'Eresby Mountain mine', which was actually the old Gwydyr Park Consols workings in Gwaith y Gors and Fucheslas. Seeing a further money-spinner they formed a new company to float this concern, offering the shares to the then shareholders in Clementina. At that time the Watson hype was still working for the Clementina shares, which were standing in the market at a good premium. Hence the D'Eresby Mountain shares were not difficult to place. What happened next was that D'Eresby Mountain really did find a lead ore bonanza, which meant that when Clementina went to the wall in 1881 D'Eresby Mountain was still working in good lead, which must have reassured the substantial number of shareholders who were probably in both ventures.

As explained above, the Clementina Company was wound up in 1881, when it passed to a new company, Gwydyr Amalgamated. Two other concerns were incorporated in this Company, the D'Eresby Consols Mining Company and the Aberllyn Mining Company. The second of these is not a subject for this volume, other than in passing, but the first one is. This was the old Gwaynllifion mine of Gwydyr Park Consols, which had re-emerged under its new colours in 1877. We will discuss D'Eresby Consols at this point and follow with a description of the last of the old Gwydyr Consols setts, that which was mentioned above, the D'Eresby Mountain Mining Company.

THE D'ERESBY CONSOLS LEAD MINING COMPANY 1878 - 1881

This concern has to be looked at from two points of view, as a mining venture or as a sharedealing 'scam'.

As a mining prospect, there did not seem to be a lot to go for. Gwydyr Consols had spent a great deal of money and effort driving the Gwaynllifion deep adit below the lodes on the High Plateau, and had met with nothing but disappointment. D'Eresby Consols made the great point of their effort, such as it was, to drive further on the E-W lode to get under one more old N-S lode of supposed riches, the Cobbler's lode, which was to make the whole exercise worthwhile. The new shareholders, however, were told that the work had been left by the previous company due to poisoning of fish in the Parc Lake from the drainage of the deep adit, rather than that the lead ore was not there in satisfactory quantity. (There was a small grain of truth in this, in that D'Eresby Consols lease of 1878 did require slime pits to be constructed to prevent any poisoning of the lake - however, if that had been the only problem there is no doubt that Gwydyr Consols would have constructed the pits themselves rather than abandon a fruitful mine.)

In the event, the management of D'Eresby Consols employed less than a dozen men for some three years at the mine. They cleared and layed a railway in the deep adit, which was driven a further twenty or thirty fathoms, and tried one or two other points in a very half-hearted fashion. They raised no ore, nor did they make any attempt to erect any dressing machinery. At the end of the day they actually do not appear even to have fully employed such capital as they did have, as they still had over £2000 in the kitty a very few months before finishing - however, this money does not seem to be accounted for anywhere when Gwydyr Amalgamated took over. D'Eresby Consols left the mine without even being sure that they had reached the Cobbler's lode, and the mine stands today - in terms of underground workings - as they left it in January of 1881.

However, as a promotion for Messrs. Watson Bros. there was a lot more to go for in dealing in the shares than there was underground. The first two flotations from the D'Eresby group of mines - Clementina and D'Eresby Mountain had met with great success in the markets, and the latter had even a substantial discovery of ore to boost its appeal. Therefore this was a time that the magic name of 'D'Eresby' was a strong force in the minds of both speculators and promoters. Watsons pushed out D'Eresby Consols and Aberllyn on this tide, while elsewhere appeared South D'Eresby, North D'Eresby and Great D'Eresby - all seeking fame by association with the successes on the D'Eresby 'mountain of lead', as John Roberts described it.

The D'Eresby Consols Company was capitalised at £12,800, and the first 'killing' came when C. B. Parry, Mine Agent and Secretary to the Company, who was undoubtably working on behalf of the Watson 'clique', sold the new company their lease for £8800 in fully paid up shares. The rest of the shares were taken up by cash customers, which left the Company with some £4000 of working capital. As explained above, this capital does not seem to have been fully employed, and there can be no doubt whatsoever that much more money changed hands in the promoter's offices than ever got anywhere near the mine. This company seemed to fail more for lack of a positive way forward on the mine than from lack of funds, which was not the usual situation.

Even though there seemed to be no worthwhile prospect in the mine, the Watsons evidently thought it worthy of incorporating in their next pot-boiler on these setts - the Gwydyr Amalgamated Mining Company.

GWYDYR AMALGAMATED MINING COMPANY 1881 - 1883

This Company was registered early in 1881, having been formed to purchase or acquire the D'Eresby Consols, Clementina and Aberllyn Companies. The proposed capital was £70,000 in £1 shares, of which 50,000 were given to the shareholders in the three companies which went to make up Gwydyr Amalgamated. Once again the Watsons were well represented, as N. F. Watson was a Subscriber, J. Y. Watson was Chairman and W. H. H. Watson was Secretary, for which he received £120 per annum. Only a further six thousand odd shares were subscribed for, and it may be a reflection of declining confidence in the D'Eresby group that these had to be sold for 10s. per share, credited with being £1 paid.

As far as work on the properties was concerned, only Aberllyn and Clementina were put in hand, while D'Eresby Consols mine was held in abeyance. Both the other two were at work for a brief period in 1881 and 1882, when almost two hundred tons of blende were raised and dressed at Aberllyn. Unfortunately the low price which blende was commanding in the market led to Gwydyr Amalgamated having to put this concern in 'mothballs' as well, and it was decided to concentrate all remaining capital and effort in Clementina mine.

The decision was made to sink the shaft a further ten fathoms, but although they had made a start on this, and had raised and washed some twenty tons of lead ore by the time of the second general meeting of the parent company in September of 1882, the shareholders were not prepared to put up necessary further capital. A special meeting in January of 1883, at which it was hoped to raise capital by an issue of debentures, met with no success at all, and it was decided during the next month to appoint a liquidator. This was the parting of the ways for the Watsons and three of the four mines in the D'Eresby Mountain group. As mentioned above, D'Eresby Consols had finished its working life before being incorporated in the Gwydyr Amalgamated

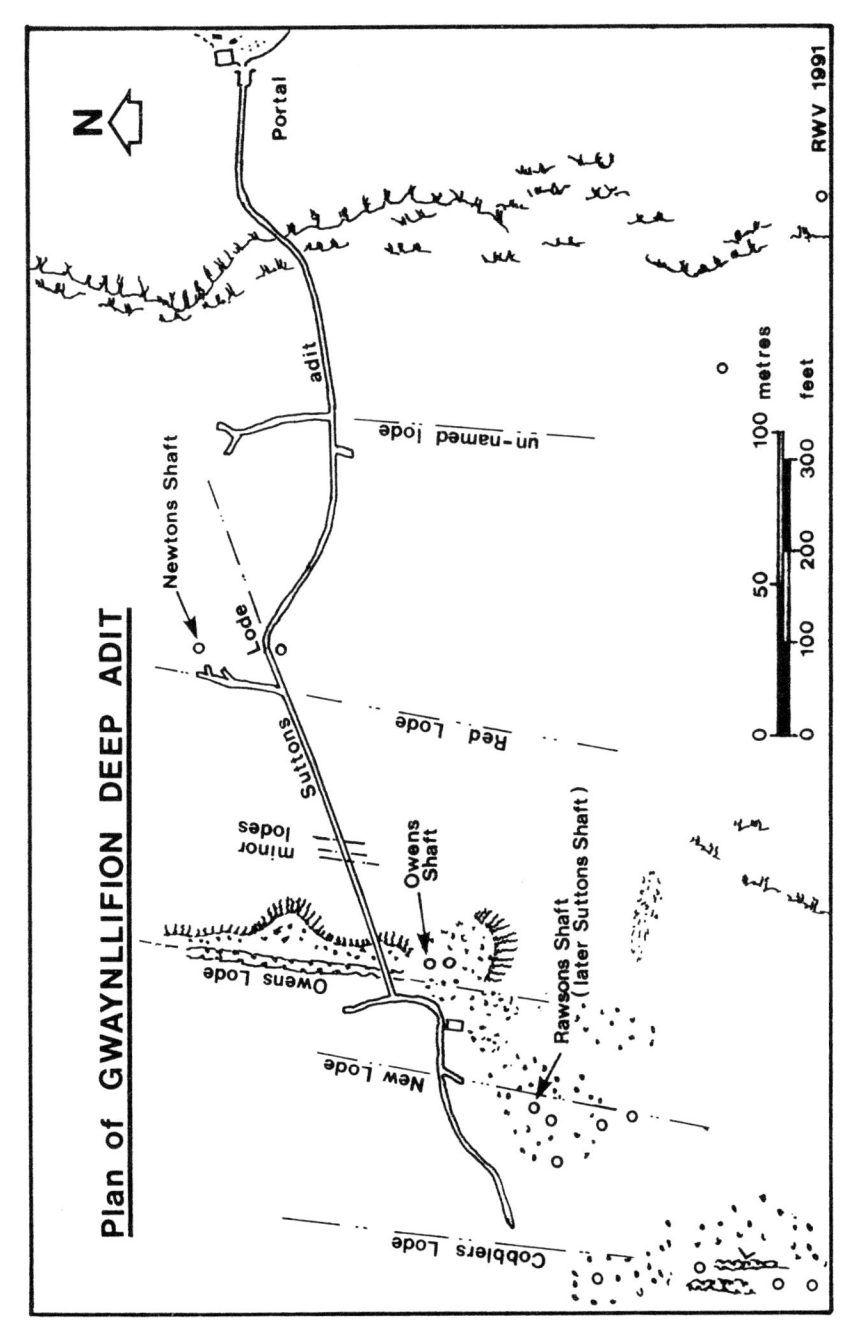

Fig. 10

Company, and now Clementina was to follow it into oblivion. Aberllyn did have a future, which will be discussed elsewhere, though under entirely new management.

This leaves only the D'Eresby Mountain mine from among those which were the components of the old Gwydyr Consols concerns. This was the apple of the Watson's eye, and we will now turn back to 1877 to trace its history.

D'ERESBY MOUNTAIN MINING COMPANY 1877 - 1884

This Company was registered on the 15th of February in 1877, with a proposed capital of £10,240 in five hundred and twelve shares of £20 each, the whole of which had been subscribed by July of 1877 by the Clementina shareholders. They appear to have had to put up a working capital of £2560 and allot £7680 in fully paid shares to the Clementina Company in payment for the concern. At its simplest this allowed the proprietors of the D'Eresby setts to raise a further £2560 in cash to work another point on their property, and gave them another company to provide director's fees, rentals, fees for secretarial work, etc., and - most importantly for them - another share to deal in.

Looking at the mine itself, one has to believe that this was probably the prime motivation in this promotion, as Gwydyr Consols had left it for dead in 1872. However, with the promise that there was a good blende lode in the No.1 level, and that the old objective of driving the Deep Adit level under rich old workings in Fucheslas still held some attractions, the D'Eresby faithful were prepared to have another go. In this they were no doubt influenced by the extraordinary success which the proprietors had achieved in 'puffing' the Clementina shares, which at that time were highly priced - and undoubtably overpriced. Prospects appeared to have been transformed in November of 1877, when Capt. Bennetts '- struck by an appearance of lead and spar in the side of the level, and his curiosity being excited, had a hole blasted, resulting in a fall of lead and the discovery of the heading of the Gorse (sic) lode'. Unfortunately for Bennetts, his reward seems to have been his replacement as local Mine Captain by William Sandoe within a few months. This was undoubtably a major find in the context of the local mines, but it was not with them that it was being compared by the proprietors - this lode compared with the mighty Van mine, was the wonder of the neighbourhood, would lead to the mine becoming one of the most profitable in Wales, etc., etc. The speculators loved this and the £20 shares touched £100 in the market. Even at that price Jehu Hitchens could work out that the shareholders could expect an annual dividend of 10% - though anticipated discoveries in the mine were expected to improve even on this prediction.

However, the development was going to be costly, and more capital would be needed immediately. Watsons first attempted to float a new company to exploit the 'Valley sett', which they had just secured for a rent of £100 per annum. In the event this did not meet with the D'Eresby Mountain shareholders approval, though they were quite happy to subscribe more capital to their company, which they did in October of 1878.

The management now set about clearing the newly acquired deep adit from the valley (the old Cors y Nant level) to get under their new discovery (which was in the old Gwaith Isa Mine). At the same time they did some work in the Fucheslas levels and on what they described as the 'Great' Hafna lode. In addition to this they set about erecting two waterwheels, a crusher and a stone breaker as well as jiggers and other dressing machinery.

By 1879, and not before some anxious prodding from at least one of the shareholders, the enterprise was beginning to get ore out of the mine and dress it, and the twenty or so men who were regularly at work in the mine were joined by a further pare of dressers. Maximum employment reached thirty-seven in 1881 and 1882, which was also the most productive in terms of ore weighing. The Gors shaft gradually became the focus of all underground work, and it became evident that hopes of rich ore being found along hundreds of fathoms in the heading of the Gors lode were not going to be fulfilled. The good ore they had discovered was, in fact, a 'pipe' of ore, which would require sinking to exploit.

Even so the management were confident that they could pay the costs of the mine from the proceeds which they would obtain from raising and dressing twenty tons of ore per month, and they were equally confident that they could raise and dress up to fifty tons a month when they got into their stride. In the event the lode proved to be more difficult to exploit than they had anticipated, the ore being disseminated over a width of lode of some sixty feet, and with the going harder than they had expected.

SUMMARY OF RETURNS OF MEN EMPLOYED AND PRODUCE TAKEN FROM THE MONTHLY RETURNS LEDGER FOR THE GWYDYR ESTATE GWYDYR PARK MINE/D'ERESBY MOUNTAIN MINE – 1853 -1884

Year	No. employed	Ore weighed	Comments
1853	10 (Oct.-Dec.)	—	G.P. Consols (cost book)
1854	10-26	—	Capt. H. Rawson
1855	2-19	—	Driving W. towards
1856	8-11	—	Fucheslas on
1857	7-11	—	Cross Mawr level.
1858	7-17	3.17.0 Pb	
1859	7-20	—	Erecting crusher
1860	19-22	48.16.3 Pb	& reservoir.
1861	6-8	4.10.3 Pb	Capt. W. Smyth took over
1862	7-10	2.18.2 Pb	in Oct. '60.
1863	7-11	4. 5.2 Pb	
1864	7-11	19. 3.2 Pb	
1865	8-11	16. 2.3 Pb	
1866	7-3	4.16.0 Pb	Standing from April
1867	2-3 (Sept.-Dec.)	—	Driving west towards
1868	2-5	—	Fucheslas.
1869	2 (Jan. only)	—	
1870	—	—	Standing, G.P. consols
1871	—	—	(limited liability)
1872	2 (Jul. & Aug.)	0.15.0 Pb	took over '70 - men
1873	—	—	at Tyn Twll.
1874	—	—	Take note Hitchen &
1875	1 (May & Jun.)	—	Sutton Oct. '74.
1876	2-3	—	D'Eresby Mountain
1877	3-17	—	Mining Co. Dec. '76.
1878	20-26	—	Gors lode discovered
1879	22-23	29.15.0 Pb	in Nov. '77.
		21. 8.0 Zn	Company opening mine
1880	27-34	49.14.1 Pb	& erecting machinery.
1881	34-37	96. 2.2 Pb	Capt. John Roberts.
		21.12.2 Zn	
1882	37-30	204. 7.0 Pb	Gors shaft to 6th level,
1883	30-20	114.18.1 Pb	but parallel
		40. 0.0 Zn	New shaft necessary.
1884	34-14	19. 2.1 Pb	Insufficient funds
		38. 1.0 Zn	to carry on.

Total Pb (lead sulphide concentrates) 1853-1884 = 614.5.0

Total Zn (zinc sulphide concentrates) 1853-1884 = 121.1.2

The D'Eresby Mountain Mining Company was replaced on the sett by the D'Eresby Mining Company in November of 1884.

Fig.11

As things turned out they only managed to raise some five hundred tons of lead ore and something over one hundred tons of zinc blende between 1879 and 1884, when the Company was wound up. By 1883 they had sunk the Gors shaft to the No.6 level, where the lead ore had been somewhat disappointing, but there had been an improvement in a sump which had been sunk below this level. At this stage it had become evident that they were not going to be able to develop the ore body without a second shaft, which would need to be sunk some sixty fathoms to get into the ore ground, and this had been commenced in 1883.

Prior to 1883 the Company had not experienced difficulty in raising additional capital, when required, from the shareholders. Indeed the shares still commanded a premium in the share market right up to the beginning of that year. However, when the sinking of the new shaft led to a steady run on resources in 1883, the first signs of serious disenchantment appeared, when not all calls were answered.

The annual meeting in June of 1884 learnt that the concern had been running at a loss of £150 per month for ten months by that date, and that it was essential that the current offer of debentures to raise capital should be supported. Sadly for the D'Eresby Mountain Mining Company this plea fell on stony ground, and on the 6th of August, 1884 a liquidator was appointed to wind up the Company.

He was able to obtain some relief for the beleaguered company when he sold the mine and plant for the sum of £2000 to the D'Eresby Company, who were to succeed them on their sett. The plant he sold to them was described in some detail in the advertisement for the sale of the old concern which subsequently appeared in the publication 'The Mining World and Engineering Record', and this is reproduced in Figure 12.

The Monthly Returns show that the mine was at a stand in August 1884, but by November there were men back stoping, clearing water and timbering the new shaft. This marked the arrival of the new proprietors, the D'Eresby Mining Company. For some reason best known to themselves the great majority of the old shareholders, who had not been prepared to put any more capital into the old company, were quite prepared to put up capital for the new company. Even though the Directors were all drawn from the old company, J. Y. Watson and C. B. Parry signed the lease, Watson was again the Chairman, the mine was the same, and the problems and proposed remedy the same, they still came up with the cash.

In Liquidation.

NEAR LLANRWST.

D'ERESBY AND GWYDYR MINE.

IMPORTANT SALE OF THE WHOLE OF THE VALUABLE MACHINERY AND PLANT.

MESSRS. W. DEW AND SON are instructed to OFFER FOR SALE BY PUBLIC AUCTION at the Mine as above (about 1 mile distant from Llanrwst), on FRIDAY, the 4th day of DECEMBER, 1891, at ELEVEN a.m., the whole of the VALUABLE PLANT AND MACHINERY, including Hammers, Drills, a quantity of best Olive, Machine, and Cylinder Oil, the contents of Smithy, Shafting, Pulleys, Bevel Wheels, Couplings, a FIFTEEN HORSE-POWER FIXED ROBEY ENGINE, as good as new, TEN HORSE-POWER SEMI-PORTABLE ROBEY ENGINE, with Spur Gearing and Winding Drum attached, 70 fms. ¾ in. Steel Wire Rope, NEW PIT HEAD 24 ft. high, with Pulley and Pedestals, PIT HEAD with 4 ft. Pulley and Pedestals, 70 yds. Tramway of T rails, 14 lbs. to the yard, Three Tramways 115 yds., with Bridge Rails, Tram Waggons, Barrows, 84 yds. of Tramway of Bridge Rails, New 30 ft. DIAMETER WATER WHEEL, 3 ft. breast : 65 fms. of 6 in. Pumps, 150 fms. of Underground Tramroad laid with T and Bridge rails. Blake's Stone-breaker, 30 - ft. DIAMETER WATER WHEEL, 3 ft. breast, CRUSHING MILL, 9-in. CYLINDER PORTABLE ENGINE, 2 ft. stroke, with Tubular Boiler, VERTICAL BOILER, three Plunger Jiggers, Chat Mill, 9 ft. Water Wheel, erection of several Wooden Sheds with Corrugated Roofs, and a quantity of Tools, &c., &c.

Township of Gwydyr, near Llanrwst, North Wales.

THE D'ERESBY MOUNTAIN MINING COMPANY, LIMITED.

IN LIQUIDATION.

MR. F. M. WHITTINGHAM will SELL, by order of the Liquidator, by PUBLIC AUCTION, at the Guildhall Tavern, Gresham Street, London, on THURSDAY, the 16th day of October, 1884, at Two o'clock p.m. precisely, according to the conditions of sale to be produced at time and place of sale, the whole of the MACHINERY and MATERIALS belonging to the D'Eresby Mountain Mining Company, Limited, together with the Legal and Equitable INTEREST in the LEASE on which the Mine belonging to this Company is worked, as a GOING CONCERN.

There will be included in the sale one 10 horse-power semi-portable steam engine, with pumping and winding gear ; winding drum ; one 30-feet diameter water-wheel ; one portable engine for drawing ; one Cornish crusher ; one Blake's stone breaker ; two sets of self-acting jiggers ; tram waggons ; kibbles ; 70 fathoms of ⅝-inch diameter steel wire rope ; pumps ; rods ; and all other machinery and materials belonging to the Company, including a variety of useful materials for the continued working of the Mine.

Held under lease from the Baroness Willoughby D'Eresby, from 30th November, 1877, for twenty-one years, at an annual rent of £100 per annum, or a royalty of 1-12th on ores raised, and an additional charge of £5 for use of reservoir.

For further particulars apply to the Liquidator, Mr. Edward Ashmead, F.C.A., 2, Drapers' Gardens, London ; Messrs. Stacpoole and Son, Solicitors, 2, Pinners' Hall, Old Broad Street, London ; Capt. John Roberts, Bryn Crafnant, Trefriw, North Wales ; and of the Auctioneer, Mr. F. M. Whittingham, 5, Bishopsgate Street Within, London.

4th October, 1884   2nd November, 1891

Fig. 12

Sales Advertisements placed in the Mining World and Engineering Record

THE D'ERESBY MINING COMPANY 1884 - 1889

The history of this concern is very much a re-run of that of its predecessor on the sett, though in a slightly grander style. They were at work for almost exactly five years, during which time they increased employment to over sixty for a time and were able to raise and dress some eight hundred tons of lead ore and one hundred tons of blende. As before they incurred heavy and on-going expense in sinking the two shafts to the ore ground, where they reached the No.9 level, and also were unable to dispense with the use of the relatively costly steam engine. As before, they had lead, but it cost more money to raise it than it fetched in the market - a problem aggravated by the general weakness in lead ore prices during their tenancy.

J. Y. Watson was again the rock on which the shareholders built their aspirations, and the strength which his presence brought was graphically demonstrated when the enterprise went into terminal decline following his death in May of 1888. However, at the first annual meeting in 1884 all was hope. The shareholders in the old Company had, by and large, forked up for the six thousand £1 shares offered to them at 10s. paid in the new Company, and drawn their six thousand bonus shares. The lease, machinery, etc. had been purchased from D'Eresby Mountain for £2000 and there was £1000 working capital in the kitty. They were stoping below the No.6 level and soon hoped to expand output 'beyond anything in the past'.

It also seems probable that the company sought to improve the potential of the dressing machinery during these optimistic times. A sales advertisement for the plant and machinery of their successors on the sett - D'Eresby and Gwydir Mines Ltd, (1890-91) - certainly gives the impression that the plant had been upgraded to some extent since D'Eresby Mountain had left, and as D'Eresby and Gwydir really never got off the ground, it is safe to assume that any investment which was made between 1884 and 1891 must have been undertaken by the D'Eresby Mining Company. This advertisement is to be seen in Figure 12.

By 1886 the new shaft had been sunk sixty fathoms to five fathoms below the No.6 level. It was lauded as a remarkably successful piece of engineering, as although it had been achieved by four pares of miners sinking or rising simultaneously, the kibble did not touch the side of the shaft anywhere during its descent to the ore ground. This development work had put the concern in the red, but this was put right by a call on the shares. This was paid ungrudgingly, as the Directors were now able to report that they had never had, at any time, such brilliant prospects. This reflected in the share market, where D'Eresby Mining shares stood at a large premium - up to £4 on a £1 share.

The mining costs by that time required the sale of some three hundred tons per annum of lead ore before there might be anything to distribute to the shareholders. The only year that they almost reached this was in 1887, when two hundred and ninety tons were weighed. This was not achieved again, and the annual meeting in 1888 was told by Capt. Dunkin of Hebden Moor Mines, who had been commissioned to present a report on the D'Eresby mine, that their redemption lay in further sinking. This must have sounded very ominous to the long-suffering shareholders, and Watson was asked some pretty searching questions before apparently deflecting his critics and being able to justify the further call for funds which was made on that occasion.

As mentioned above, his death in May of 1888 was the last straw, and it was obvious that the stuffing had been knocked out of the company both physically and financially. The shares, which had stood at £5 a couple of years before, fell to a nominal 5s., while work at the mine itself virtually came to a halt while direction was sought. One unfortunate shareholder who had bought at the top wrote '- to say that the shareholders are completely disgusted with this state of affairs would be a euphemism'.

The Directors did make some effort when the dust had settled after they had lost their Chairman, appointing a new Mine Captain in W. H. Williams and commissioning a report from Captain Henry Nottingham. The money which had already been subscribed before the demise of J. Y. Watson did enable them to sink to the No.9 level and raise more ore, but they were still working at a loss, which led to the final collapse of the company. Unhappily the affair ended in mutual recrimination, not only between the directors and the shareholders, but also Captain Williams was accused of lack of attention to the mine and criticised for his advocacy of rock drills, which were held to be inordinately expensive, while Captain John Roberts caught it for not developing the mine in a competent fashion. Roberts in turn accused the proprietors of never providing sufficient capital. A sad story in all respects.

However, the D'Eresby promoters were still not completely finished, and C.B.Parry still found it in himself to subscribe to a new company, D'Eresby and Gwydir Mines Ltd., to take over the concern which D'Eresby Mining had left - including their debts and liabilities.

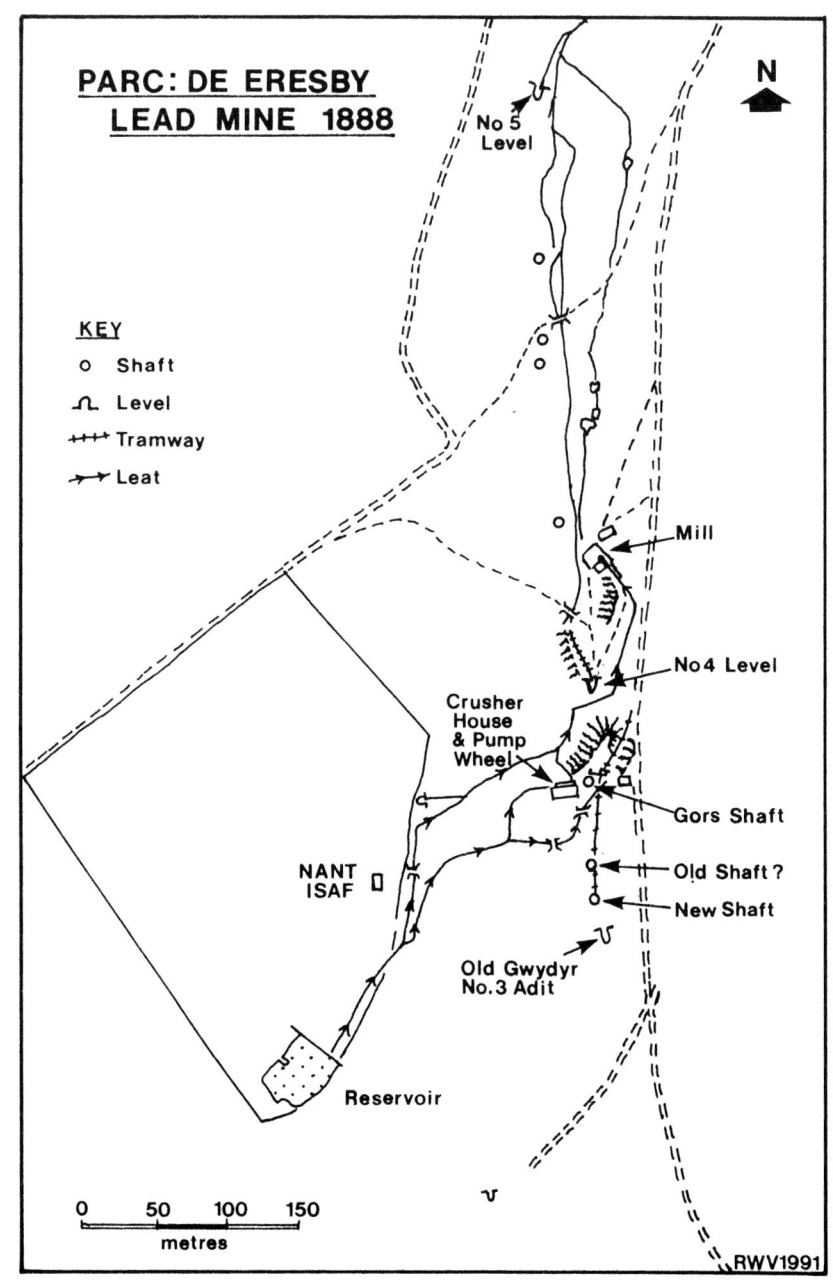

Fig. 13

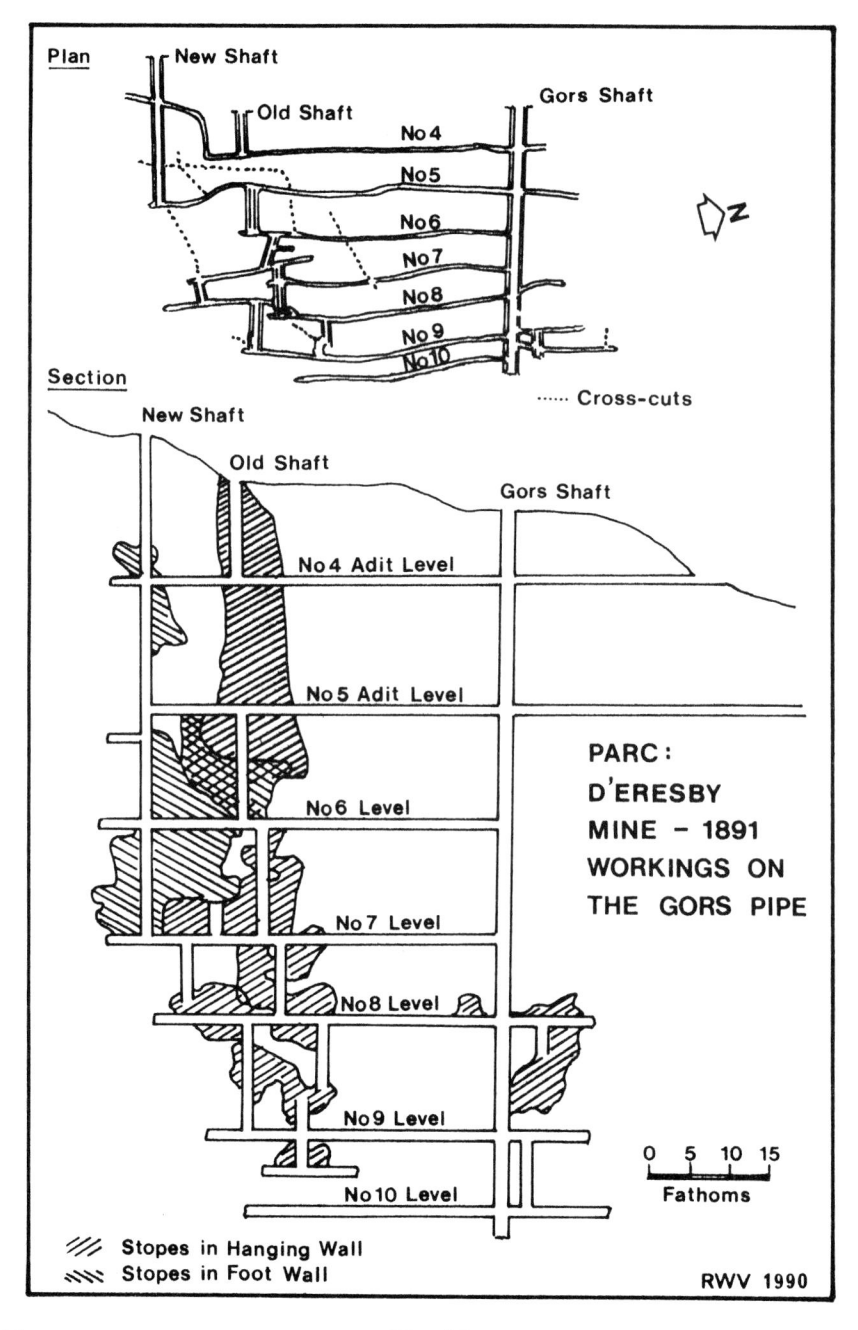

Fig. 14

D'ERESBY AND GWYDIR MINES LIMITED 1890 - 1891

The new company appear to have purchased the shares in the old company for sevenpence a share and offered shares in the new company on a one-for-one basis - £1 shares with 17s. credited as paid. Working capital to emerge from calls on the outstanding 3s. per share. This met with some success and enough capital was raised to make a start on the mine.

Employment during 1890 reached a maximum level of over forty men, who were engaged both in working in the lower levels in the mine and extending and making good the reservoir. The object of improving the capabilities of reservoir and waterwheels, as a cost saving exercise, was successful, but the efforts of the men underground was less so. At the first annual meeting in August of 1891 the shareholders pressed the Mine Captain, Henry Nottingham, for details of production costs. He was forced to admit that he was only able to promise in the order of five tons of lead ore per month, and that costs ran ahead of income on that basis. As one shareholder put it 'We spend £100 to get £50'.

Like many others who had found themselves in similar circumstances in similar ventures, the Mine Captain believed that with the expenditure of a further £1000 he could turn matters round. On the basis of this the directors felt justified in resolving to issue a further 10,000 shares of 3s. each share. Also not surprisingly the offer was not subscribed, and the concern was placed in the hands of the Liquidator in September of 1891. The advertisement for the sale of their property is reproduced in Figure 12, alongside the D'Eresby Mountain sale, and one may notice a minor increase only in sophistication in the plant which the later company had employed.

The last word on the matter was to come from John Roberts in a letter to the Mining Journal in November of that year. It was his belief that had the Directors followed out the proposals he had made, '- the mine, instead of being in liquidation, would today have been in a flourishing condition.' It was no fault of his, he claimed, nor of the mine. There were rich points that only he had seen, and 'he would be glad to confer with any intending purchaser.' The concern was to be taken up again a year or so later, though more for blende than lead ore, and the incoming proprietors did not see fit to take up Roberts on his kind offer.

SUMMARY OF RETURNS OF MEN EMPLOYED AND PRODUCE TAKEN FROM THE MONTHLY RETURNS LEDGER FOR THE GWYDYR ESTATE D'ERESBY MINE/PARC MINE – 1884 to 1920

Year	No. employed	Ore weighed	Comments
1884	14 (Oct.-Dec.)	—	D'Eresby Mining Co.
1885	21-22	54.18.1 Pb	from Nov. '84
		23. 8.2 Zn	Sinking New shaft
1886	29-30	120. 6.0 Pb	on Gors pipe
		9. 5.0 Zn	Capt. John Roberts.
1887	43-63	289.16.3 Pb	
1888	63-64	175.16.3 Pb	J. Y. Watson d'd May.
		24. 5.1 Zn	Capital expended in
1889	64-8	135. 1.1 Pb	sinking shafts on
		15.12.1 Zn	Gors pipe.
1890	8-30	60.13.0 Pb	D'Eresby and Gwydir
		6. 4.2 Zn	Mines Ltd. lessees.
1891	36-2	62.17.0 Pb	Liquidated Sept. '91.
		7. 7.3 Zn	
1892	2	0.18.3 Pb	
		1.19.1 Zn	
1893	18-24 from Aug.	—	Parc Lead and Zinc
1894	24-33	4. 6.2 Pb	Mining Co.
		24.13.3 Zn	
1895	25-47	37. 6.1 Pb	Principal effort to
		214. 8.0 Zn	mine zinc, but not able
1896	47-24	40. 3.1 Pb	to work at a profit.
		261. 3.1 Zn	
1897	12 Jan.-Apr.	—	Co. left in Apr. '97
1898	10-38 May-Dec.	—	Brunner Mond May,
1899	38-105	161.10.2 Zn	trying for zinc ore
1900	96-103	65.19.2 Pb	various points.
		173. 7.2 Zn	Not satisfactory -
1901	30-3	—	men at Aberllyn.
1902-June	1905 caretaker	—	6 men on tribute 1905
1905	6-25 from July	—	C. R. Holmes takenote
1906	30-2	28.16.3 Pb	'05 succeeded by
1907	6-44	—	lease '08 to C.R.H. Co.,
1908	12-0-22	125.18.3 Pb	Llanrwst Consols.
1909	8-26	61. 4.1 Pb	
1910	6-30	126.18.3 Pb	Trying Fucheslas &
1911	18-30	190. 0.2 Pb	Parc Intermediate
1912	6-30	32. 5.3 Pb	levels - Principal
1913	30-8	35. 1.1 Pb	olde. Employing
		152. 2.1 Zn	air driven drills.
1914	8-12		
1915 & 1916	No returns		
1917-1920	2-12	—	Prospecting

END OF RETURN

Total Pb (lead sulphide concentrates) 1885-1920 = 1632.18.1
Total Zn (zinc sulphide concentrates) 1885-1920 = 1075. 7.3

Fig. 15

THE PARC LEAD AND ZINC MINING COMPANY 1893 - 1897

Nothing much had happened in 1892, with a couple of men looking after the pump under the supervision of Captain Nottingham. However, in November of that year a take note for the concern was let to one William Boundy. Boundy was a metal merchant from London, and he was one of the seven subscribers to the Parc Lead and Zinc Mining Company, which was registered in July of 1893. Other subscribers included members of the Phillips and Board families, both of which had sharebroking connections.

By 1892 both lessees and lessors were obviously conscious of the problems which beset this type of enterprise, with almost all Gwydyr mines at a stand, and the new company was offered a complicated royalty agreement, which fell to 1/16th when metal prices were sufficiently depressed.

Even so, the venture did not meet with much success, only operating until May of 1897. The issued capital was £4222 out of a total capital of £5000. How much of this went in discounts to attract buyers for the shares, or how much on purchasing the concern in the first place is not clear, though the latter should not have been a lot, as they were operating a new take note from the Estate, and not buying an existing lease. We do know that they spent money on a new engine, and that they generally had to pay wages for anything up to forty-seven men. We also know that they managed to spend all their capital, plus the income from the sale of nearly five hundred tons of blende and eighty-odd tons of lead ore, and furthermore get themselves into a debt of £4215.

This was the first company for some time on this sett not to put all its effort into the Gors pipe, and their principal interest was evidently in mining blende, the value of which had increased substantially during the 1890s. To this end they must have re-opened the upper levels on Craig Fucheslas, while elsewhere it seems likely that at least some of the lead ore they weighed came from Kneebone's Cutting, which first appears on the maps and plans drawn by Kneebone in 1899. Whether he was employed by the Company in a managerial capacity is not known, but he certainly spent time in the mid-1890s writing eulogies to the Mining Journal on the subject of the Gors lode, both in Parc mine and Aberllyn mine, at the second of which he was a joint leaseholder from 1894 to 1897. After the Parc Lead and Zinc Company left in May of 1897 the mine was at a stand for about eighteen months, but in November of 1898 a big player appeared on the scene, both at Parc and also at Aberllyn.

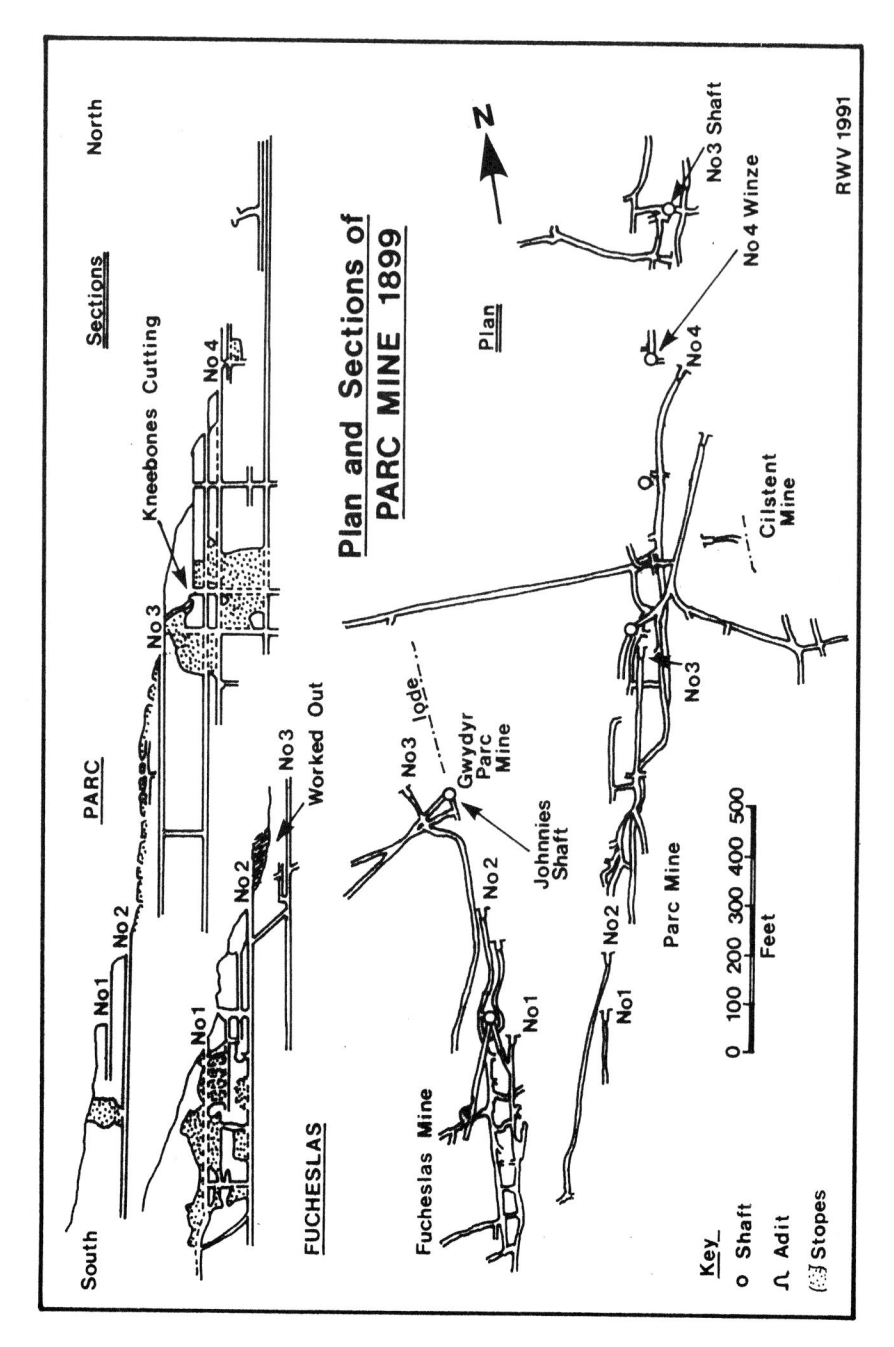

Fig. 16

BRUNNER MOND & CO. LTD. 1898 - 1905

Messrs. Brunner and Mond had established their chemical works in Northwich, Cheshire, in the year 1873, where their principal business was the production of soda ash. The principal by-product of the ammonia-soda process which they employed was calcium chloride, and by the end of the nineteenth century they were seeking methods to recover chlorine from this compound. In pursuit of this end they sought to decompose calamine (zinc carbonate) in the presence of the calcium chloride. To secure supplies of raw material they acquired leases for a number of mines in North Wales, where they both re-worked old tips and mined new ores. The mines were mainly in the Mold area, but did include Parc and Aberllyn mines in Gwydyr, with the project being under the supervision of C. E. Bainbridge and Captain Kneebone.

Messrs. Board, Boundy and Phillips sold the Parc lease to Brunner Mond & Co. for the sum of £3000, where the new company took possession in November of 1898. Evidently Boundy et al had procured the Aberllyn lease, in addition to Parc, late in 1894, and this was also assigned to Brunner Mond the next year, the new owners taking possession in 1896. When the property granted to the new company was drawn together in a single lease in 1899, the area covered was as much as five hundred and four acres, which made it much the largest enterprise that Gwydyr had seen.

At the peak of activity, in 1899 and 1900, Brunner Mond had over four hundred men at work on the two setts put together, though Parc generally saw only about a quarter to a third of the number employed at Aberllyn, and the men were taken out of Parc some time before Aberllyn was left. It was also at Aberllyn that a new mill was constructed, though the mill which had been employed by the previous proprietors at Parc was also put to use.

As mentioned above, it was the zinc ore which brought Brunner Mond to Gwydyr, and between November, 1898 and July 1901, when the company ceased any activity in the Parc Mine, they raised over three hundred tons of blende and sixty-odd tons of lead ore. To effect this, and to carry out their development programme, they raised employment figures from ten at the end of 1898 to over a hundred through much of 1899 and 1900. When they dismissed seventy-five men in November of 1900 they were left with twenty-six to carry on development work, but this had fallen to a single caretaker by July of 1901.

In the Aberllyn mine the statistics were substantially higher, with over three hundred men employed for a time, and with over one and a half thousand tons of blende weighed, plus a few tons of lead ore. The proprietors also persevered for a longer time in Aberllyn, not suspending mining until July of 1904.

In common with the Parc Lead and Zinc Mining Company which had preceded them, and being interested in zinc ore not lead ore, Brunner and Mond paid no attention to the Gors pipe, which was partially flooded. They did explore the winzes on the Gors lode to the north of the Gors shaft, and a cross-cut east on the No.3 level in search of the Shale lode, and also - more significantly than they appreciated at the time - they extended the Fucheslas No.2 level to reach an E-W lode, which they did not name. This was, in fact, what came to be known as the Principal lode, and it was the source of many times more ore than all other parts of the mine put together.

However, Brunner Mond had not cut the lode at a good spot, and it did not carry much zinc ore in any case, so it was left. Elsewhere the developments were not sufficiently promising to encourage them to carry on, with de-watering the Gors pipe not being thought worthwhile, and with added complications arising from relatively low grades of ore and problems in dressing.

They did strike a contract in March of 1905 with Messrs. William Lloyd and Moses Owen, of Ffrith Cottage, Nant B.H., to raise and dress ore on tribute. Lloyd and Owen, who were described as Labour Contractors, were to raise and dress ore and deliver to Llanrwst Station, for which they paid Brunner Mond a 25% royalty. Nothing much can have come of this, however, as Brunner Mond surrendered the lease on the 10th of May, 1905. They were very soon replaced on the sett by Charles Holmes, a colourful character from America, who held the lease for over twenty years.

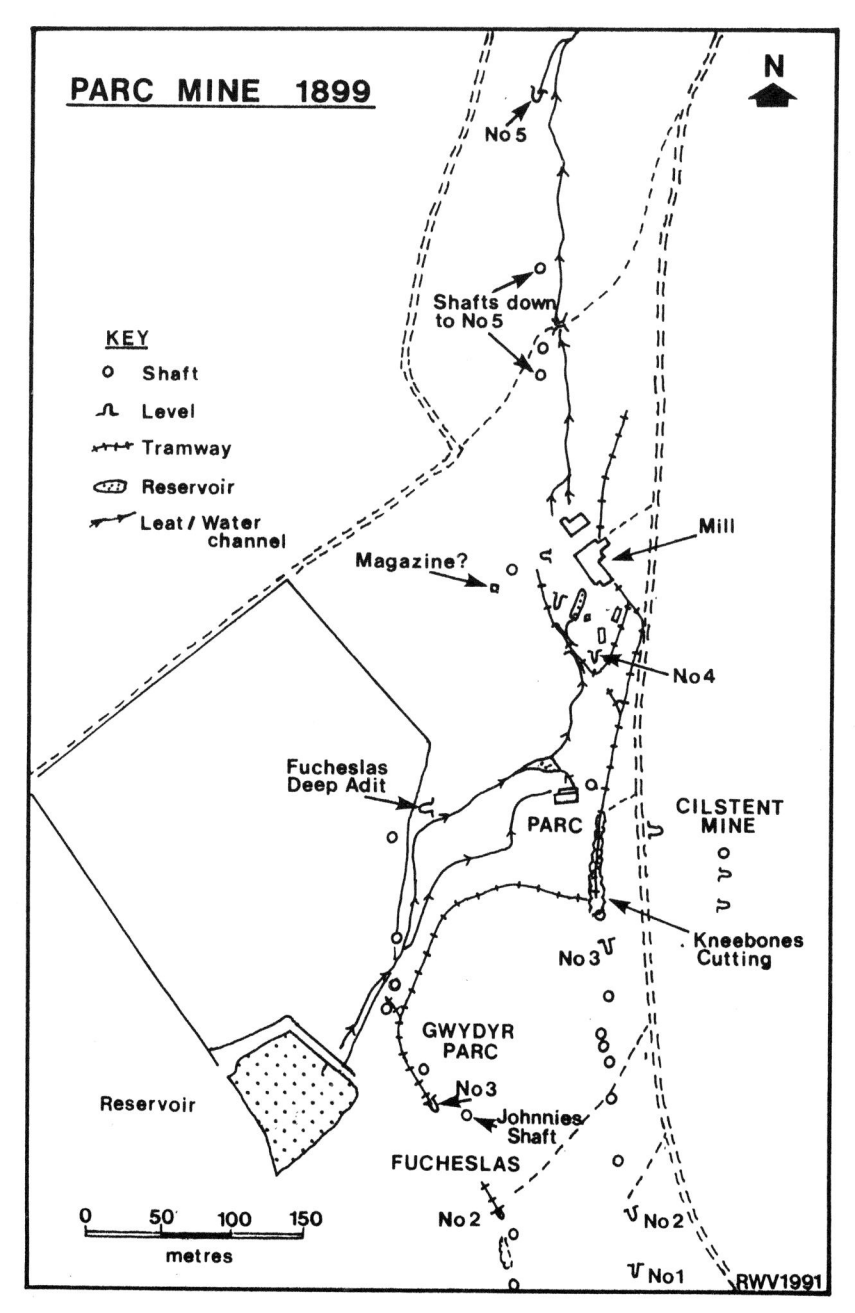

Fig. 17

C. R. HOLMES.
LLANRWST CONSOLIDATED MINES LIMITED

Charles Robinson Holmes, a practical engineer from Butte, Montana, came on the scene in 1905, when he obtained a three year take note on the Parc, Llanrwst and Gorlan setts, which he subsequently converted into a twenty-one year lease. He came to England in the first place as an employee of London United Tramways, though he evidently had some previous experience of metal mining, when he had been employed as an engineer at a mine in Butte - a large mining centre at the turn of the century.

It was in 1908 that he formed the Llanrwst Consols, of which he was always to remain very much the principal shareholder. He did not make much of the enterprise, working the mine in intermittent fashion, and only raising in the region of one thousand tons of lead ore, plus a little blende, during the twenty-five years in which the mine was open under his direction. However, he did leave us with graphic descriptions of his time in the area, both his efforts in Parc itself, and the people with whom he had to deal. His experience with the 'hot-air mining engineer' in 1917 has already been described in volume one of this series.

> He described his first trip to the Gwydyr Forest as follows - *'I wandered all round the district and viewed many holes in the ground and the debris removed therefrom. There was no activity going on except for a couple of men working with hand steel and wheelbarrow on the Gorlan sett. They were taking out a little ore which contained a rib of galena from one inch to one and a quarter inches wide, which they were breaking up with hammers and hand jigging at intervals. This did not seem to me to be a very suitable process for operating any mine. No compressed air drills, with which I had been familiar at Butte, Montana, had ever been used anywhere in the district and I knew that one of these would get out more rock in half a day than the two men could do in a week, working with hand steel and single-jacks. I was amazed when I looked over the many and large dumps of refuse which had been brought out by such methods and could quite understand why mining in that locality had not been profitable. I could not see how it had ever been accomplished, even when I learned that miner's wages were only £1 per week for forty-four hours!*

As Holmes said - he thought he could do better. To which end he approached Gwydyr Estate Office and obtained his three year take note. He evidently contemplated the possibility of de-watering the workings on the Gors pipe, where the Agent had told him that the only substantial ore body in the mine had been found. This would have meant pumping out in the region of a million gallons of water, which flooded the mine for three hundred and sixty feet below the natural drainage level. In the event this project was not embarked upon, as Holmes was able to speak to an ex-Manager of Parc (or D'Eresby mine, as it would then have been known) who had been in charge when the Gors pipe had last been worked, and who persuaded Holmes that the ore in this part of the mine had been exhausted.

The part of the mine which did attract his attention was the lode which Brunner Mond had intersected at the end of the Fucheslas No.2 level, which they had not named, but which was now described as the Principal lode. They had cut the lode at a bad place for mineralisation, and, after driving a few fathoms west and still being disappointed with the appearance, they had left - leaving the rails in place which had been laid to the forebreast in the level. Holmes had soon chosen his initial point of work on this lode, taken on his men, and installed modern air driven drills - he was soon in trouble with all three of these choices.

Holmes first set-back came very soon after he had started his effort, when he discovered that the rock in the Principal lode was very hard indeed, and the air drills which he had purchased were wholly inadequate to the task. In addition to this he found the sharpening of the drill bits a headache and, when by sitting down and designing his own drills and bit sharpeners he overcame those problems, he found that the steel continually fractured in the drill holes. This turned out to be a problem associated with the hollow drill steel which had just then become the vogue - so he then set out successfully to develop a satisfactory method of hardening the steel.

With all these difficulties finally behind him came the problem with the men. As Holmes put it, they believed that these drills had been given to them to make it easier for them to produce the same amount as they had by hand steel, rather than to enable them to actually do a bit more per shift. He put this to rights by giving them what he termed his 'take it or leave it' contracts. These boiled down to paying them £4.10s. per fathom driving and £2.5s. per square fathom for stoping. They generally achieved about 2ft. progress each day and were able to make a satisfactory living on these terms.

The last problem was the persistently poor grade of the ore, which dogged the enterprise throughout its life. Holmes saw himself chasing an inch wide

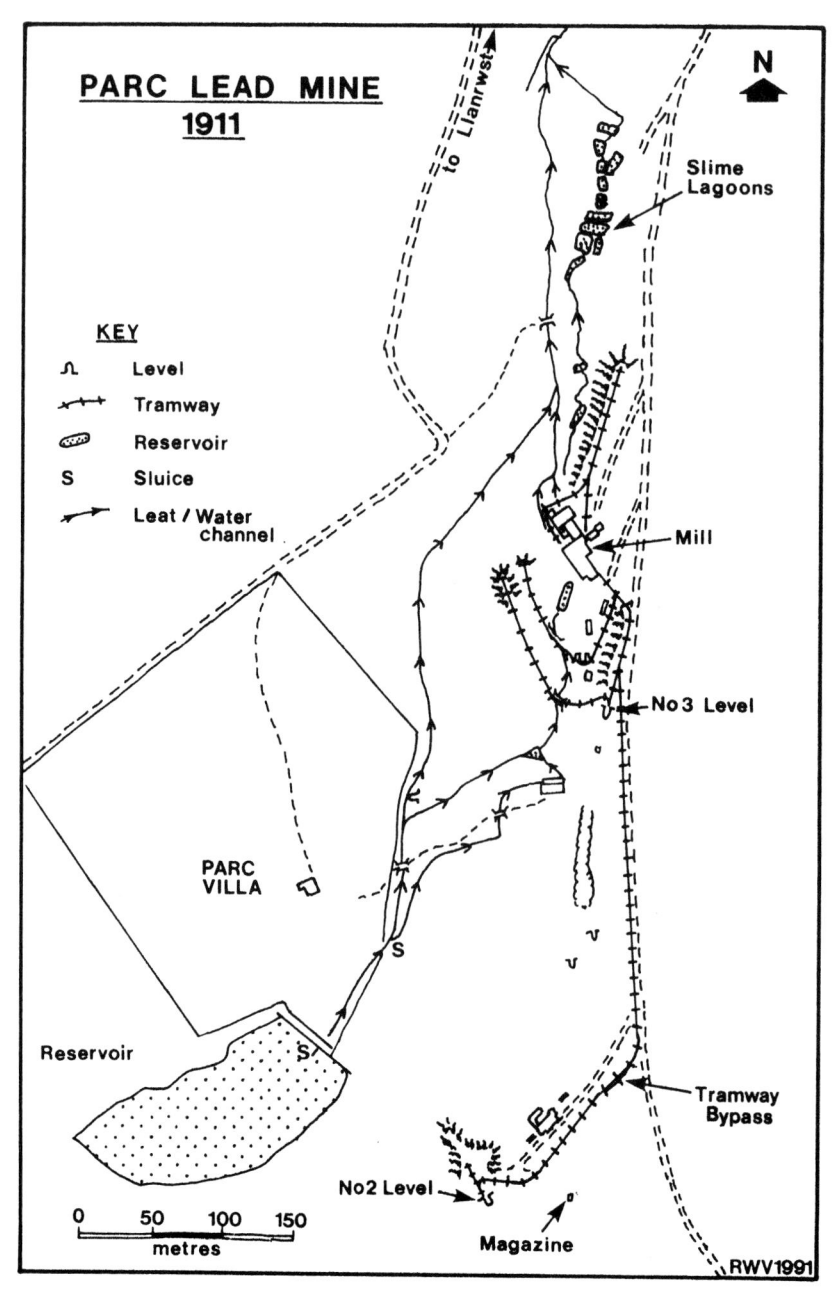

Fig. 18

rib of galena through the mountain for the rest of his life, which he found a discouraging thought.

Between 1905 and 1912 Holmes kept his job going in London, putting the day to day affairs of the mine in the hands of a Manager. During the first two years he tried a local man, then a mill man from a nearby copper mine, then a German from the Vielle Montagne Company, then a young graduate from the School of Mines and finally a man who answered his advertisement in the Mining Journal.

He was not satisfied with any of them, and even found it necessary to ask an old friend who was a retired private detective to keep an eye on them. At the end of the day he appointed a young engineer from London with no experience of mining whatsoever. He filled the place admirably until Holmes left his job in London to take up residence in Gwydyr in 1912, when the two worked together for some time. Holmes was a man who liked to do things his own way, and it well may be that the young man, Murrin, was the only one who knew little enough about mining not to offer to contradict his boss.

Holmes soon decided to establish a base in the area, and the problems he got into with two of his frequent sparring partners - the local Council and the local community - are best described in his own words.

> 'In early 1908 I desired to build a house on the mine and wished to do so of log walls, there being any amount of suitable trees available on the Gwydyr Estate at 6d. per cubic foot. The house I had in mind would have been single storey with six rooms, bath and scullery, a very attractive structure very popular in the towns and country of Western America, warm in winter and cool in summer; the little spaces between the logs filled in with cement mortar, the logs being, of course, clean peeled and the outside varnished; very nice to look at.
>
> I found I had to submit plans and specifications to the Local Council and get their approval. I prepared the necessary and went to see the Surveyor, who, at sight of what I intended, went straight up in the air with an emphatic NO. That would never do; unheard of; unprecedented; and could not be entertained for a moment. The walls would be combustible and a death trap for the occupants, beside being a dangerous fire hazard for the neighbourhood. He produced a book of rules and regulations; a massive volume; obviously copied en bloc from

the laws of Liverpool or Manchester, where such might perhaps have some sense, but none whatever on Parc mine. Any house I built would have to conform strictly to every one of the silly rules. There was nothing for it but to conform; hence Parc Villa as you have viewed it.

It cost me £440, including stoves in every room; linoleum throughout and window shades. If I could have built a better one of logs the expense would have been less than half as much. Carpenters wages were 27s. a week at that time and common labour 22s.

One Saturday, some years after the house was finished, I had occasion to need a couple of cart loads of tailings brought up to the Villa, for use first thing on Monday morning and arranged with my carter to come up Sunday morning and do this; he being a renegade Welshman who regarded time-and-a-half for Sunday work more alluring than religious devotions.

About 10.30 next forenoon, as I sat in the dining room with the north window open, I heard a great hullabaloo going on over at the main road and looked out. The loaded cart had just entered the field, and along on the road side of the wall was a line of twelve or fifteen men and women, all yelling and shouting and gesticulating wildly. I was mystified as to what this was all about until the carter arrived and reported that the frenzied ones, headed by the pastor, had come along in procession on their way to the chapel and were incensed at the sacrilege on the Sabbath which the carter and I were committing; taking time off from their progress to curse and execrate the two of us in about equal proportions, and at length.

The carter had responded with corrosive repartee, which had not soothed the tumult. When my elderly Welsh housekeeper returned from the chapel at the top of the Nant, she was literally seething with fury against me, and mentioned that the Minister had devoted his entire sermon to my atrocious conduct and in his prayers had implored the Lord to destroy me and the carter by a rain of fire and brimstone or by lightening at his option; either method being quite satisfactory, so long as a thorough job was made of it and the Nant was purified. The saintly parson had worked himself up into a real passion. He had also advised my housekeeper to immediately leave my detestable employ, an intended bomb-shell which proved to be a 'dud' when I expressed utter nonchalance, flavoured with derision.'

Parc Villa was to remain a useful home for company personal for over half a century after Holmes had built it.

The mining enterprise was by no means active all day and every day. Only for a part of the time would Holmes have the men at work in the mine, driving, stoping and stock-piling ore. When enough ore for a decent run of the mill had accumulated the mine would be shut down and the ore dressed. However, the concern was frequently at a stand altogether while Holmes argued with the men, the local Council, or anyone else who incurred his disfavour. Even he seemed to be a little surprised that however often he dismissed his workforce, they always came back when there was something to be done.

One of the features which appear on maps of the mine is the incline tramway, which Holmes used to get his ore down from the No.2 level to the mill. He described it as follows –

> 'This was one track, with a double track for a suitable length in the centre so the cars would pass; the loaded car pulling the empty one up.
>
> The wire rope was ⅝" diameter of coarse wire and went around a deeply grooved pulley wheel at the top which had a powerful lever brake with wooden shoes attached. The galvanised iron rope required only one and a half wraps round the pulley to give sufficient friction when the brake was applied to enable the cars to be stopped exactly where desired. This rig worked first class throughout and I guess I opine it lowered about ten thousand tons of ore. The said pulley wheel was 4ft. in diameter.

Holmes also left a detailed description of the mill as it was when he had it working. He had found it 'practically complete', and from what he wrote, it seems that Brunner Mond, from whom he purchased the machinery, had further upgraded the old 'D'Eresby and Gwydir' plant of the mid-1890s. The introduction of a series of trommels, and possibly some addition to the jigging facilities, allowed Brunner Mond to achieve a more sophisticated classification of the partially milled material.

One piece of equipment which Holmes did introduce was the Wilfley Table, as he mentioned in his account below:-

> 'After the trams were emptied into the ore bin at the end of the track it was trammed across the bridge and dumped on the floor, where it was hand-fed into the stone breaker (5" by 15" opening). After crushing

it dropped onto a shaking trough which bumped it along to a set of Cornish rolls, 16" face and 30" diameter. After passing these the stuff went into a revolving trommel, 24" diameter and 72" long, with 7mm round holes.

The stuff which passed through these holes was laundered through the wall to the four central jigs, which had 7, 5, 3 and 2 millimetre round holes respectively. The oversize from the primary trommel was laundered through the wall to an auxillary set of Cornish rolls, 12" face and 24" diameter, in the west part of the jig room and thence was carried by bucket elevator to the floor above and into a revolving trommel with plate holes 6 mm. diameter. From there it went into four Hartz (German) jigs with plates having 6, 4, 3 and 2 millimetre round holes.

The waste from both sets of jigs was laundered to a bucket elevator in the N.W. corner of the jig room and discharged into the waste bin, from which it was hand trammed to the tailings tip. The 'chats' deposited in the last compartment of all jigs were hand carried to a set of small 'chat' rolls in the east side of the jig room and, after re-crushing, went up on a bucket elevator to sizing trommels, and thence to two chat jigs in the N.E. corner of the jig room.

The slimes were laundered down to a Wilfley table in the north room of the mill. Originally there was nothing in this room but a round buddle, of which I did not think much, for it took too much labour to handle the stuff. All was well after I installed the Wilfley, which I bought second hand at a derelict copper mine in the north of Anglesey.

The power was supplied by a 60HP undertype Robey engine, compound, 150lbs. per sq.in. This was not quite powerful enough, owing mostly to the demand for power by the primary crushing rolls, but all went well after I made up a condenser for the L.P.exhaust system.'

Holmes also described an additional source of power which he was able to tap.

'On the east side of the mill, and close alongside, was an overshot waterwheel, 30ins. face and 30ft. diameter, which at some time in the past had probably operated jigs in the mill. When I took hold it was not connected up in any way to the machinery, but when I built the galvanised iron covered store room immediately east of the waterwheel, I put in shafting and a 6ft. diameter pulley inside the store room,

'Thunderbolt Charlie' Holmes at the age of eighty-three. The nickname was given to him by those who witnessed his driving of the steam wagon with which materials were carried to and from Parc mine.

connected to the waterwheel, and belted its power onto the main line shaft inside the jig room. This gave some added power, and was worth doing, as it saved some fuel.'

Holmes was able to mill two tons of ore per eight hour working shift, or eleven tons per forty-four hour week, when there were no interruptions, though there were evidently many of these for a variety of reasons. During his first ten years he had, in fact, only managed to raise and dress some seven hundred and fifty tons of lead ore concentrates and about one hundred and fifty tons of zinc ore concentrates. (See Figure 15) This, by his own estimates, had necessitated milling the ten thousand tons of ore which had been trammed down the incline. He had only sought to establish galena content in his ore by the most arbitrary methods, and had come up with a figure of eight and a half per cent - so this was not too far out of line with his other approximation.

When the concentrates were ready for sale Holmes only had the choice of two smelters in this country, one in Chester and one in Swansea. He clearly felt that they took some advantage of this situation in their dealings with him, and he even sold off some small lots to London agents of overseas smelters - at least before the war - however, he never fell out with them about either weights or the regular 2oz. per ton silver content in his material.

Work in the No.2 level ceased during the first world war, when the Ministry of Munitions pressed an interest-free loan of £1200 on Holmes to encourage him to seek to increase his production of lead ore to support the war effort. Holmes had explained to the Ministry that his best hope of assisting them would be to drive the No.3 level beneath the point that he was working the Principal lode in No.2 level. In the event the lode was not as productive at this point as had been hoped, and there is no evidence that Holmes met with any increased success. In fact, the end of the war saw men back in the Fucheslas levels and prospecting elsewhere in the mine.

There is no evidence to indicate that after the war the mine met with much success, and Holmes had ceased mining completely by 1929. He was not encouraged to start again when the price obtained for pig lead slumped in 1930, and it did not pick up again until 1936, when rearmament gave metal prices a boost, but when Holmes had already been back in America for four years.

Many years after Holmes had gone from Parc he wrote as to why he stayed as long as he did, and why he finally left. For the first he blamed over-development of his triple bumps of stubbornness, obstinacy and optimism, though the last had been severely deflated before 1920. As for his leaving, he wrote that he left the mine intact in the hands of an agent to wait for better times. These, he wrote, came in 1936, when he sold to the 'Kenya Company' (Watende Ltd., previously Watende Mining (Kenya) Ltd., the abbreviated title having been assumed in 1936) for a sum which saved his financial skin.

However, there is some evidence to show that the concern was actually placed in the hands of the liquidator when he left for America in 1932, and when there were mortgages to be repaid. Dawson Ware, who looked into the concern pretty thoroughly, dug out accounts to indicate that by 1928 Llanrwst Consols was showing a loss over the years in excess of £6000, and that the valuation of machinery in the books at over £9000 was a gross exaggeration of its worth. It seems possible that the lease, machinery and any other assets changed hands once or twice in the early 1930s, and were finally sold to the Watende Company for the sum of £4000 in 1936.

WATENDE LTD. 1936 - 1942

This company leased the Parc sett for £35 per annum, which was the same as Holmes had paid without the added Llanrwst and Gorlan setts, but, in addition, they were required to pay a 4% royalty on the ore they weighed. The management was placed in the hands of William Mitchell and Charles Evans, the latter having previously managed the nearby Cyffty mine operations. They concentrated their effort on developing the Principal lode in the No.3 level, plus some stoping above the No.2.

During the years 1936 to 1938 they brought some five thousand tons of ore to the mill, from which they produced a little over five hundred tons of lead concentrates. However, they were still employing the old gravity mill from Holmes day, which suffered from a poor recovery rate, making for unprofitable operation when taken in conjunction with the poor prices which governed at this time. They set out to dismantle this plant in December of 1938, and there was a pause in operations until new plant was commissioned in 1940.

The flow sheet in Figure 19 shows the mill procedure as it was in 1942, at the end of Watende's active period. As mentioned above, the surprising feature of this process was the lack of use of the flotation technique, which had been widely adopted elsewhere many years prior to the construction of this mill in 1940.

Even with the improvements that this mill brought (see below), the problem of a high pyritic content in the zinc concentrates still existed. Again, the answer to this seemed to be use of flotation plant, which was suggested at the time (Robertson), and we will see below that the Company sought financial aid to install such plant. However, this was not obtained, and it well may be that it would not have proved a redemption, as their successors on the sett, Llanrwst Lead Mines, were no more successful in producing at a profit than they were, although they did employ the flotation technique.

As mentioned above the Company sought to extend their mining and milling operations quite extensively in 1940. To enable them to finance their proposals additional to the new mill they approached the office of the Non-Ferrous Metallic Ores Committee, a body which had been formed to advise the Ministry of Supply as to where they might best make government grants to increase necessary production of raw materials to assist the war effort.

It was recognised by the officials of the Non-Ferrous Mineral Development Control - evidently a body which was associated with the above-mentioned Committee, that Watende were holders of very substantial reserves of ore. They noted that production was at a low level, and the concern was bedevilled by problems of finding skilled men to operate the mine and the mill, as well as a chronic shortage of water to keep the mill at work on a continuous basis.

They had already examined a proposal from the Company in pursuit of the hoped-for grant, in which considerable drivages on both Gors and Principal lodes were proposed - should the necessary cash become available - as well as a sinking a new inclined shaft on the Principal lode and providing for extensive re-equipment with winding engine, new wagons and electric loco, installation of power line, new rock drills, a second mill and a flotation plant - a total of some £35,000 of investment.

However, the advisers to the Ministry were not able to make a good enough case to interest the Ministry in making a grant either then or later, when, with Japan entering the war, Watende evidently thought it might be worth a second effort to attract their financial support.

On this second occasion they were much more modest in their suggestions about capital investment, stating that £2000 would enable them to obtain necessary mine cars, rock drills, etc., but they did admit that even with this they would only be able to mine and mill at a loss, and they invited the government to subsidise their production costs to the tune of £5 per ton. This would, even then, only enable them to cover their costs. They were no more successful on this occasion than on the former, and the next year saw the Watende board seeking to sell plant and lease to yet another body, this time described as the Non-Ferrous Metals Development Company, though with no success.

However, while all this was going on behind the scenes, the new plant commissioned in 1940 had put them in a position to achieve an immediate increase in production, and they were able to weigh off thirteen hundred tons of lead concentrates, plus over two hundred and fifty tons of zinc concentrates during the years 1940 to 1942. The lead concentrate was over 80%, but the zinc only 33%. During 1941, which appears to have been their best year, the Intermediate, or No.3 level, had been driven over two thousand feet west from the intersection with the Gors lode. During that year there were six stopes being worked, sixteen hours a day, by a total of twenty-four miners - evidently two men per stope working in eight hour shifts. In the absence of the hoped-for electric locomotive the ore was trammed two thousand feet by pony to the adit by the mill, using what few mine cars they had.

They were able to achieve a weekly output of ore from the mine of 5,170 cubic feet on average. The cost of milling this material, after rough sorting underground, was between 15s. and 20s. per ton, while during five and a half eight hour shifts in the mill they were generally able to produce ten tons of lead concentrates and up to five tons of zinc concentrates. In the mine the driving costs in the heading were on average 38s. per foot, and they could attain eighteen feet per week, which was a slight improvement on Holmes's efforts. They considered that they had some 44,000 tons of this relatively low grade ore available in the Principal lode.

This was not good enough to merit carrying on, and the mine was left standing from 1942 until 1949, when prospecting by a new company led to the enterprise being resurrected once more - for what was the last time prior to the time of writing, and what may prove to be the last time - full stop. However, before passing on to these new proprietors it is worth recalling the interest which had been shown in Parc mine by Dawson Ware of D. W. Holdings.

This company has already been met in an earlier volume (volume two), when as lessees of Hafna and Pandora during the 1930s, they were seeking to interest support for drawing together all the principal ventures in the Gwydyr Forest. They did not succeed in this objective, though Dawson Ware was still a 'player' until the late 1940s. Among the projects with which he sought to attract capital to the area was a 'master plan' involved the driving of a deep adit to get under all known ore bodies, when he estimated that 3,517,000 tons of payable ore would be available. Parc was to provide a mere 999,000 tons out of this total.

LLANRWST LEAD MINES LIMITED 1949 - 1958

The years after the second world war saw British lead and zinc mining at a very low ebb, and in July of 1949 the Mineral Committee of the Ministry of Fuel and Power reported as follows:-

> *'There are at present no important proved reserves of lead and zinc ores in England and Wales, and if the industry is to be revived it will be necessary for new prospecting and exploratory work to be put in hand. We believe that there are areas in this country where favourable results might be expected.'*

One company which accepted the challenge was the Johannesburg Consolidated Investment Co. An account of their years at Parc is found below, and, at the end of the section, there are some additional notes on the method of working which they adopted in the mine, and on the operation of the mill.

J.C.I. made use of the experience they had acquired on their South African properties using what was then the 'state of the art' diamond drilling technique.

They applied this method at Abbeytown in Ireland and at Matlock in Derbyshire as well as at Parc mine, and the attendant good sample recovery made possible an accurate assessment of the ore percentages in the lodes which they intersected. The drilling programme at Parc was preceeded by a geophysical survey which defined the limits of their main field of interest, which was the Principal lode.

PARC MINE

This photograph of the horse-drawn wagon emerging from the haulage level was taken during the period of activity of the Watende Co. The young man in the school cap is the late Robert Taylor Clough, who was to become a prominent figure in the field of historical mine research and recording.

After a preliminary report by W. W. Varvill in 1949 plans were made to thoroughly investigate the prospect, both by the drilling programme and by exploration and the taking of samples from the existing workings in Parc mine, as well as seeking to prove other areas of mineralised ground away from the Principal lode. To effect the former an initial six boreholes were planned at intervals over a distance of 5700ft. of the Principal lode. As far as the latter was concerned, the company were fortunate in having access to reliable mine plans and sections, as well as being able to enter the Watende workings, which had only been left some few years previously.

The boreholes were being drilled through 1950 and 1951, and the company were satisfied before the last hole was completed that there was sufficient potential to open the mine. The results established a probable average 5.8% lead and 2.0% zinc ore content in the lode, and Varvill's report of July, 1952 made the following predictions of reserves.

SUMMARY OF ESTIMATES OF ORE RESERVES			
PRINCIPAL LODE	PROVED	170,357 tons
	PROBABLE	80,983
	PROSPECTIVE	434,342
GORS LODE	PROVED	13,224
STOCKPILE	PROVED	10,714
	TOTAL TONNAGE	709,620

To which add extensive dumps containing ore rich enough to warrant milling under present day conditions of price and recovery.

While these more elaborate investigations were being pursued with the diamond drills, the company was also going over the ground and the old workings carefully. This side of the business was in the hands of Arnold Taylor, who was to be described as mine captain in 1952, and who graduated to manager in 1956. He paid attention to the old Gorlan deep adit and also particularly to the Cyffty deep adit, which was to be thought of as the 'back door' to the mine in future years - a possible way out if trouble arose.

In addition he scouted other areas at surface, being especially interested in the old Ffriddllechwedd workings adjacent to the Llanrwst mine, and to the outcrop which occurred at the bottom of the Nant by the Grey Mares Tail waterfall - an area which had not really attracted any attention since Park Mawr was prospected during the early nineteenth century.

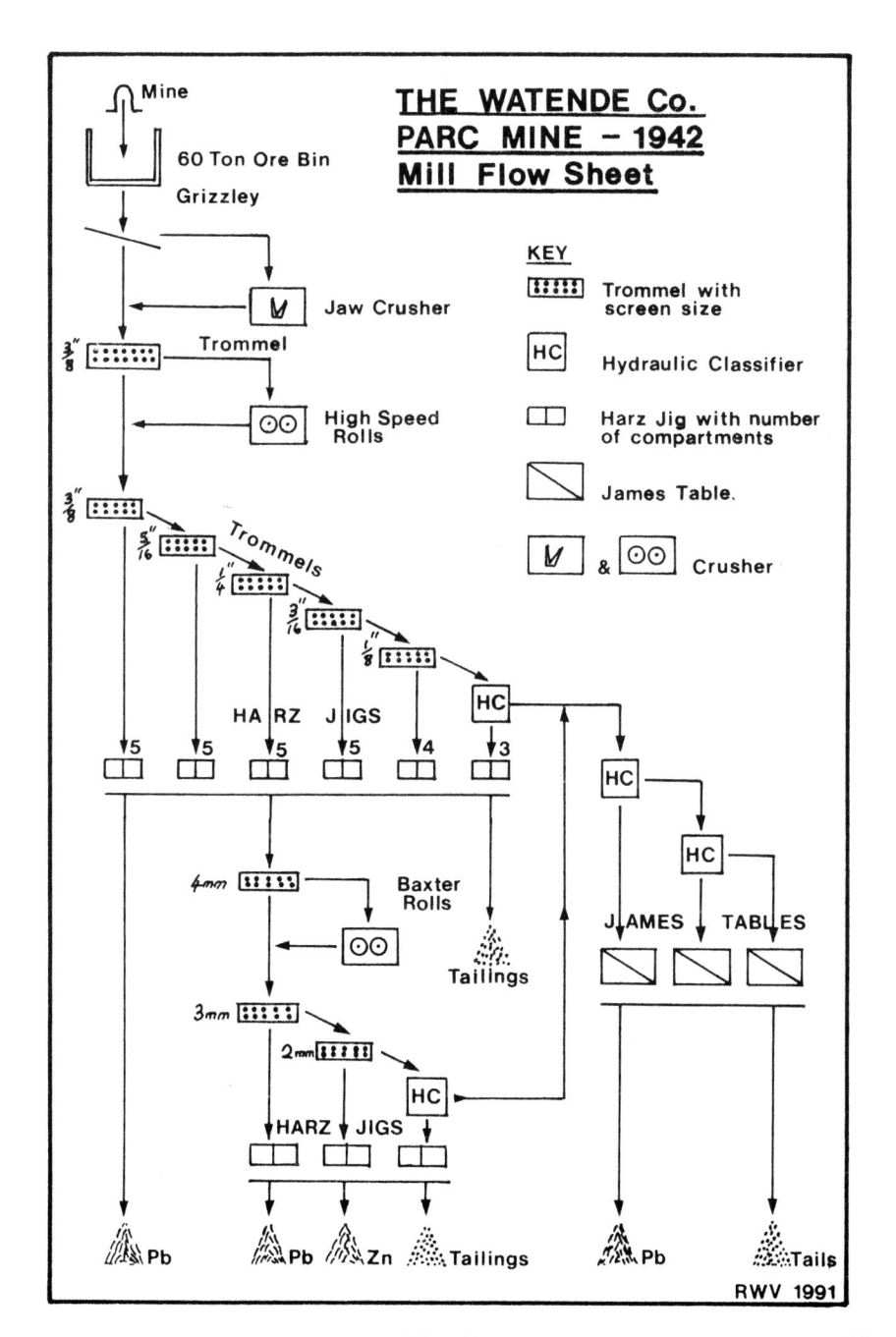

Fig. 19

On the basis of these results Johannesburg Consolidated acquired a lease to a Parc sett which was extended to cover most of the mining setts on or around the area of the Principal lode, and to exploit which they formed a subsidiary company. This was the Llanrwst Mines Limited Company, and we are fortunate enough to have sufficient written accounts of the mine to be able to trace its history in some detail - in part from the annual reports made by A. A. Archer of the British Geological Survey, and in part from the correspondence between Messrs. Varvill and J. B. Dennison, who were Consulting Engineers employed by the parent company.

Excerpts from these sources are listed chronologically below.

May, 1951. — Lease assigned by Grimsthorpe Estate to Llanrwst Lead Mines on 25th of May.

February, 1952. — Underground effort up to this time had concentrated on driving on the Principal lode. During this phase the minor splitting of the lode, which has already been described in the section on the various lodes in the area, came to notice, when the southern branch was mistakenly driven on in the No.2 level for a short distance - as mentioned above this came to be known as Mugs lode! The men were soon returned to the Principal lode proper, which lay some thirty feet to the north, where it was between four and five feet in width.

To improve efficiency in the mine a loop drivage had been driven at the intersection of the Principal lode and the Gors lode, and a new track laid in the No.3 level. It had also been necessary to widen out the main galleries, especially those on the main haulage level, so as to accommodate the 20 h.p. diesel locomotives and the larger three ton mine wagons which were now in use alongside the smaller one ton wagons. In addition, mains electricity had been laid to the mine.

June, 1952. — Between July 1951 and the end of June 1952 over 12,000 tons of ore had been extracted from the mine and put in the stockpile. The mill was now almost ready, and finally the flotation process was being brought to Parc - many years after it had proved itself to be such an improvement on the earlier techniques for extraction and concentration of the ores. The mill is described separately, and in some detail, in a section to be found later in this volume, after the history of the working in the mine.

During the second half of the year the first concentrates were finally produced, with the mill soon achieving six days work each week. The company now set about contracting for sales, sending samples of the lead concentrates to several potential customers, including H. J. Enthoven at their Darley Dale works in Derbyshire, to the Metallgesellschaft A. G. Braubach smelter in Frankfurt-am-Main and Messrs. Capper Pass & Son Ltd. However, it was Associated Lead Manufacturers who eventually signed the contract, which envisaged delivery of 200-250 tons per month to their Chester works.

Llanrwst Mines anticipated production of 100-150 tons per month of zinc concentrates, and these were contracted for sale to the National Smelting Company works at Avonmouth.

March, 1953. — Driving was continued west on No.2 and No.3 levels on the Principal lode. The Bryn Eisteddfod lode had been cut in the No.2 level and followed for a few feet. At this horizon it only contained quartz, and was left.

In the mine itself two eight hour shifts were worked at this time, with a single shift on Saturday morning, while Saturday afternoon and Sunday were reserved for maintainance work.

March, 1954. — The westward drive on the Principal lode had been continued, and the No.2 level had reached Llanrwst mine, where an incline rise had been driven up to the Llanrwst mine 14 fathom level. Ore production had been mainly from the Principal lode during the previous twelve months, where a further drilling programme had been commissioned to prove the lode 250ft. below the existing workings. It was further proposed to sink a shaft at the intersection of the Principal and the Gors lodes to 500ft. below the existing workings. On the lode itself the No.3 drivage had been established in the footwall, and Eimco loaders were being used to load the ore from the stope into the wagons.

Elsewhere, some ore had been raised from the Fucheslas lode, and exploratory driving in Rothman's adit on the Bryn Eisteddfod lode sought to prove further ore ground.

The workings in the region of the intersections of the Gors and Fucheslas lodes with the Principal lode, and the relationship to the other lodes in the immediate area are quite complex. In Figure 22 the most important features

Fig. 21

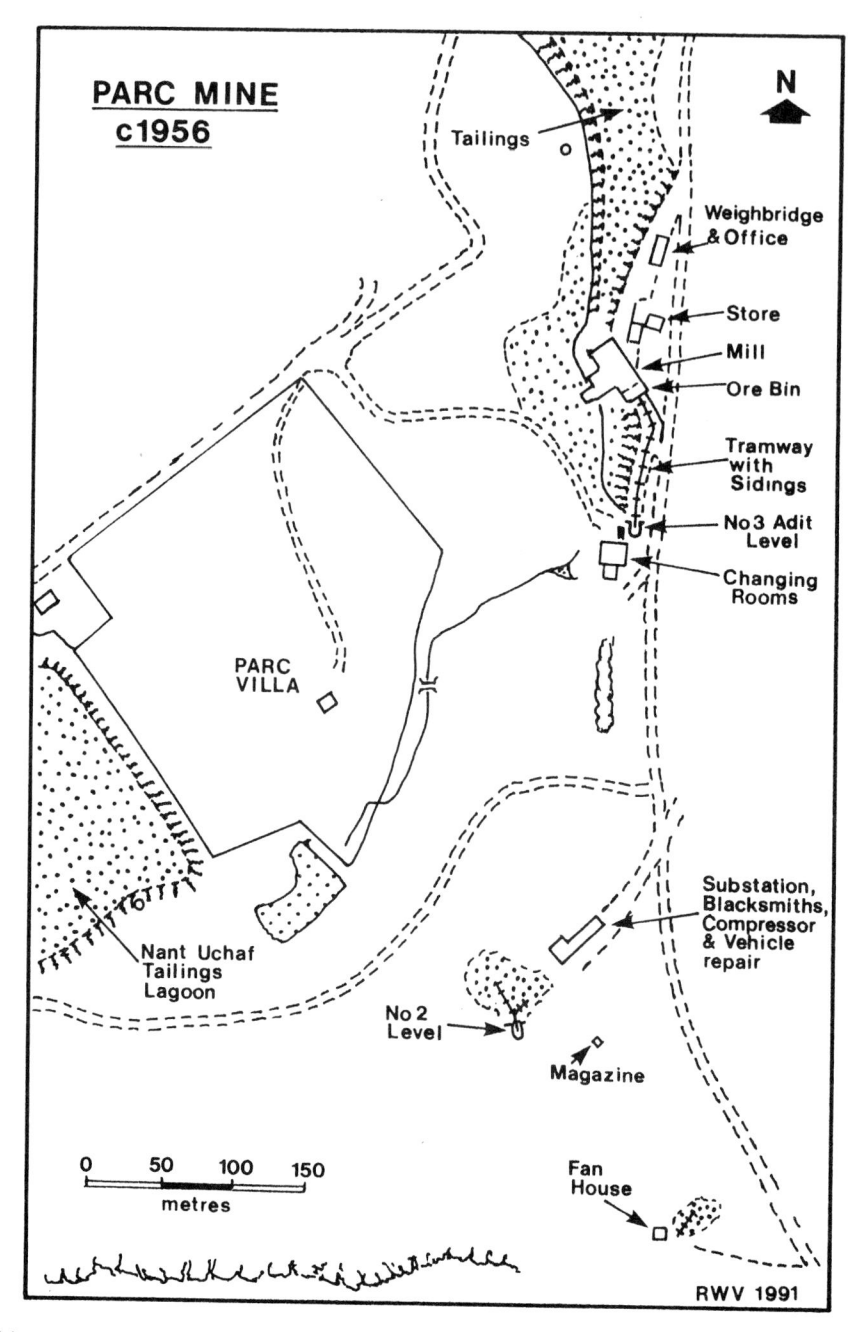

are illustrated, though a later cross-cut from the No.3 level towards the junctions of the Fucheslas, Hafna and Diagonal lodes, which was driven in 1956, has not been added, as the picture would have become over complicated. This figure reproduces the one accurate survey of the Cross Mawr level which has survived. It was driven during the middle of the nineteenth century, when the proprietors of the day drove west on the Reservoir lode, with the intention of cutting the Fucheslas lode at a depth at which it had not then been seen. The workings were evidently lost to view by later surveyors, as it is represented in later-day maps by a suspiciously straight line.

July, 1955. — By this date the No.3 level had reached and been driven beyond the intersection between the Principal lode, on which it was being driven, and the Gorlan lode. The Gorlan lode had displaced the Principal lode a short distance, and it was necessary to drive on the former to regain the latter. This point in the mine proved to be unstable, and it was necessary to rock bolt and to reinforce the locomotive route with steel arching. After the mine was abandoned there was a considerable fall here, which blocked the level completely.

It appears that the lead and zinc percentages were not as good in the Principal lode to the west of its intersection with the Gorlan lode, with an increasing pyritic content in the ore. It may have been on account of this that after this intersection had been passed the shrinkage stoping technique was adopted in the No.3 level, as this made it easier to maximise ore removal from the stope.

Elsewhere, as planned, the Parc underground shaft had been sunk in the footwall of the Principal lode at the eastern end of the mine, and a No.4 level had been driven west on the Principal lode 110ft. below the No.3. This level had been driven for 270ft., but the lode had proved disappointing, consisting mainly of vughy calcite.

The worsening of the Principal lode both in driving west and in depth, coupled with the fact that the throughput to the mill was steadily increasing, led to a down-grading of proved reserves to ten months anticipated demand from the mill. This was not improved when the ore beneath the Llanrwst mine workings was found to be unworkable.

In an effort to improve both mining and financial prospects a further series of three boreholes were sunk in search of ore, while efforts were made to find a

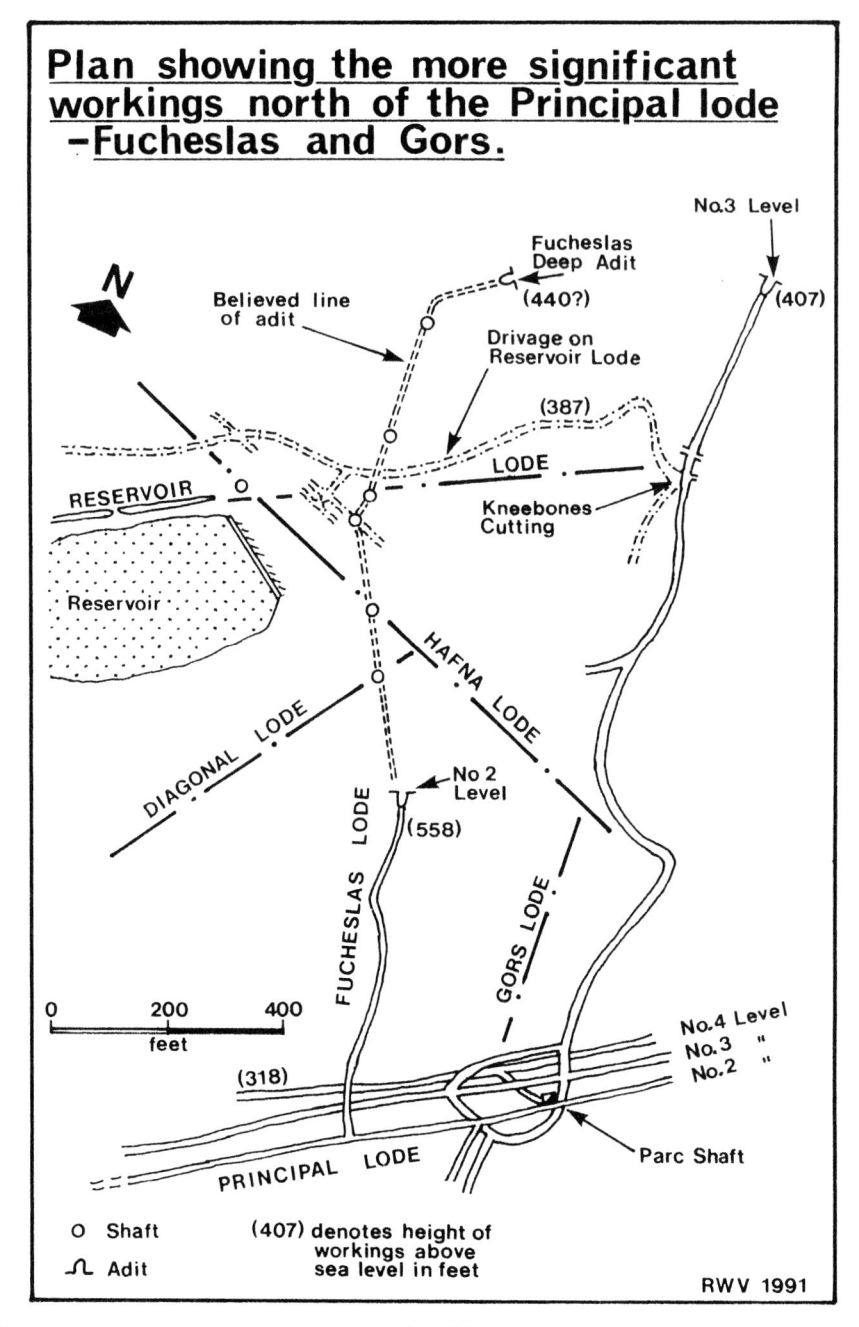

Fig. 22

purchaser for the mine waste, which was thought to be a potential material for the manufacture of bricks. This suggestion, which was resurrected when the mine was 'in extremis' some three years later, was not to meet with any success.

In 1955 one hundred men were employed in the mine, and a further seventy-five at the mill.

August, 1955. — The manager, Mr. Peter Gray, was concerned about the reducing potential for the mine which followed on the poor results obtained in the No.4 level. At that time he estimated reserves of 200,000 tons above the No.3 and 240,000 below the No.3 level. Consideration was given to driving north on the Gors lode and to working the No.1 level. The latter was not considered practical due to difficulty in moving the Eimco loaders to this point.

September, 1955. — The No.3 level had now been driven 700ft. beyond the Gorlan lode, but only 100ft. had been in payable ore. They were employing three shifts driving on the this level, in a effort to keep up the ore supplies to the mill, and driving costs amounted to £75 per day. Dennison did not think that this was the best approach, and suggested that two of the shifts be taken away and put to driving the No.2 level and to further sinking of the Parc underground shaft. It was also decided to defer an order which had been made for a double drum 75 h.p. mechanical winder for this shaft. This had been ordered from Metropolitan Vickers for the sum of £8198, but a delay in confirming the order was a mixed blessing, as the cost of the winder would be increased by £1200.

In a continuing effort to delineate new bodies of ore in the adjacent area Gray gave instructions that the Pool mine deep adit should be cleared and access obtained, and the Pool mine be examined and sampled. Further boreholes were also to be drilled in the Cyffty section of the main mine.

October, 1955. — Preparations were in hand to pump the Cyffty workings out to the 25 fathom level, when it was then proposed to put up a rise from the No.3 level in Parc mine to connect with the Cyffty 10 fathom level. When the connection was effected it was intended to allow Cyffty to flood to the 10 fathom level again. In the event there were problems pumping out the Cyffty shaft, and when the drivage from the Parc No.3 encountered a substantial stream of water, it was decided to allow the mine above to drain in this way for the time being, rather than go to the trouble and expense of pumping.

Fig. 23

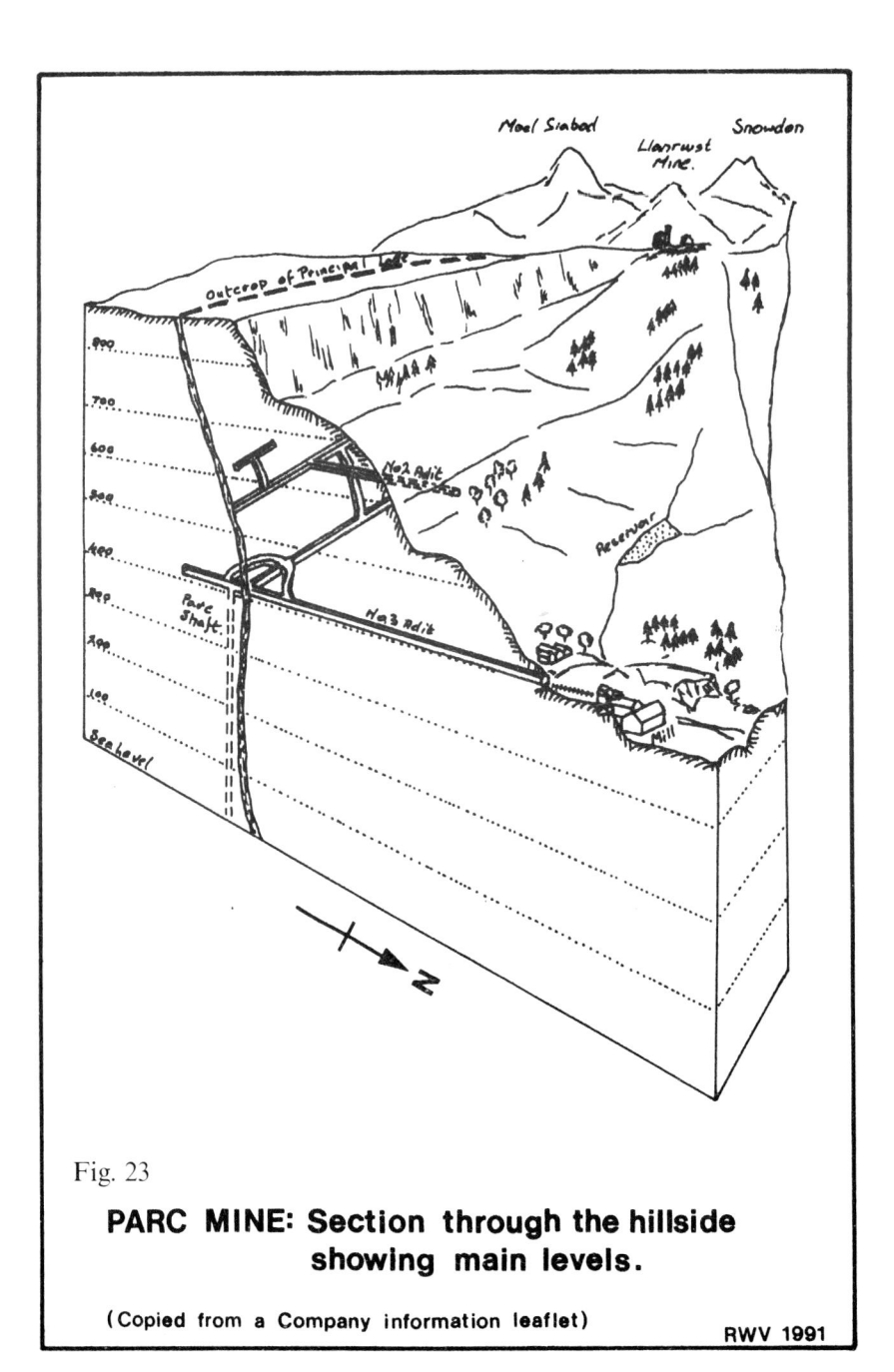

PARC MINE: Section through the hillside showing main levels.

(Copied from a Company information leaflet)

Elsewhere drivages east and west of the Parc underground shaft on the No.4 level were still encountering poor ore grades, while the shaft itself was only 9ft. below the No.4 level. Although prospects did not seem encouraging at this time the management were considering spending a further £4450 on two new locomotives, twenty wagons and a compressor, with the idea of expanding ore production to push the mill to its maximum capacity of 450 tons a day. At the same time they would spend an additional £28,000 on development, which would involve driving 3300ft. on a proposed No.5 level.

December, 1955. — Prospects improved at this juncture, when the No.4 level was driven into payable ore at the intersection of the Principal and the Gors lodes. Elsewhere, in the western end of the mine, rises had been made from the No.2 level into the old Gorlan workings, and from the No.3 level into the old Cyffty workings.

April, 1956. — This month saw the departure of Peter Gray as manager, and his replacement by Arnold Taylor, who had been associated with the project since its earliest days, and had been assistant manager to Gray. This may have been brought about by some differences which had appeared with regard the running of the mine, when Dennison, the consulting engineer, had not agreed with Gray's suggestion that - rather than embark on the expansion which was being discussed in 1955 - they should cut the workforce and abandon the No.2 level.

In an effort to expedite exploration of the Cyffty workings a contract was made early in 1956, with Messrs. Isler & Co., to carry forward the drainage programme. This was achieved, after a problem with a blockage in the Western shaft had been overcome. There is no evidence, however, that any ore worth speaking of came to light.

May - December, 1956. — While they were still able to send substantial tonnages of ore to the mill, it was clear from the returns of concentrates that the ore was becoming progressively poorer. Nor did they encounter any great good fortune in their prospecting in and around the Principal lode. It was deemed necessary to give up the No.5 level, though hopes were held for a winze which would be sunk to the No.6 level. Elsewhere they drove a cross-cut off the No.3 level to reach the intersection of the Hafna, Fucheslas and Diagonal lodes.

1957. — This year saw a small decline in delivery of ore to the mill, though a slight improvement in the tonnage of lead and zinc concentrates weighed.

However, it was becoming evident that reserves were being exploited at a much greater rate than they were being proved for the future, and the writing was on the wall.

CONCENTRATES WEIGHED AT PARC MINE – Jan 1955 to July 1958

Year	Lead Concentrates	Zinc Concentrates
1955	2957.2 tons	1397.6 tons
1956	2620.3 tons	916.2 tons
1957	2908.7 tons	1043.1 tons
1958	844.7 tons	372.6 tons

The drivage on the No.2 level Principal lode west of the Gorlan intersection was encountering poor ore, while the connection with the 10 fathom level in the Cyffty mine, which was finally secured this year, did not lead to any more encouraging discoveries. The No.3 level was now under the old Cyffty mine, but the Principal lode was starting to split. There were now only occasional patches of good lead ore worthwhile stoping, while there was an increase of marcasite, quartz and calcite in the lode.

The Parc underground shaft, which had reached 220ft. below the No.3 level, was now allowed to flood to the No.4 level, as exploratory work and drilling below this had only demonstrated that the lode comprised thin and barren stringers.

In an attempt to identify further bodies of ore the company explored both the Gors lode and the Hafna lode, where it could be found in the mine. In the former they drove south from the No.2 and the No.3 levels on the Principal lode, though the Gors lode ceased to justify further driving on the No.2 level well before it had reached the ground proved to the south by the Gwaynllifion deep adit in earlier years. However, the drive from the No.3 level did get to within a hundred feet of this point, though, once again, nothing worthwhile was uncovered.

On the latter, the Hafna lode, samples of ore were not encouraging, and the problems of the management here were compounded by what was an unusual complaint in Gwydyr - tenants in the nearby Forestry Commission properties were unhappy about the underground firing twice a day in the neighbourhood of their homes. At the very end of the year the men broke into old workings on the Reservoir lode.

PARC MINE

The Tippler House above the Ore Bin and view over the Mill and Stores Compound, showing the store and office building and the concrete approach road. The flagpoles were put up for the Queen's Coronation, and the Welsh Dragon and Union Jack were often flown for important visitors.

PARC MINE

'In' and 'Out' tracks between the mine portal and the Tippler House above the Ore Bin. The Mine Captain's Office is on the right and the Weigh-bridge Hut and Loco Repair Shop on the left.

PARC MINE

An Ore Train at a passing place in the No. 3 Adit. The heavy roof support was not normally required in Parc.

PARC MINE

Cornish-type Chutes for discharging ore from the shrinkage stopes. The figure with his back to the camera is Peter Gray, the Mine Manager.

PARC MINE

Eimco Loader discharging ore from a draw point.

PARC MINE

Cover illustration – a timberman in the Principal lode above the No. 3 level.

PARC MINE

The 125,000c.f.m. fan installed on the Air Shaft above No. 2 level adit to ventilate the mine workings. This was used only exceptionaly, as in normal atmospheric conditions natural ventilation was quite adequate.

An ore train which has just emerged from the haulage level – note how the portal has been enlarged since the Watende days.

February, 1958. — Another major factor had now come into play at Parc, where the fall in lead and zinc prices - from £114 to £73 per ton in the case of lead, and from £104 to £64 per ton in the case of zinc - meant that the poor ore which they had been milling over the previous period could no longer be treated with any hope of profit.

Manpower, which had already been reduced somewhat from the busiest days during the mid-fifties, now fell sharply from one hundred and thirty-two to fifty-seven, of whom only thirty men were working underground. They were to concentrate on four exploration and development headings;

i) Drivage west on the Reservoir lode in No.3 level,

ii) Drivage north west on the Hafna lode in No.3 level,

iii) Drivage west on the Principal lode in No.3 level,

iv) Completion of an inclined winze on No.4 level.

No stoping was to be undertaken, but the 22,000 tons of broken ore in the mine were expected to keep the mill going for some five months albeit at a reduced rate.

When this last pile of ore was dealt with the project was effectively at an end, and in July the following letter was sent to the Consolidated Zinc Corporation and to Associated Lead Manufacturers, who had been the recipients of the Parc ores from the outset.

18th July, 1958

Dear Sirs,

Owing to the low prices for zinc/lead on the London Metal Exchange, which have been ruling for some time now and do not look as if they will improve, we have not been able to continue production at our Parc Mine on a profitable basis. Milling ceased this week and apart from a few further deliveries to your works during the next few days we regret that we shall have to stop deliveries.

Should prices improve and look as if they will become stabilised we will give serious consideration to reopening, a process which will not take very long as the mine is being put on a care and maintainance basis.

Much as we regret this decision we are afraid that we have no alternative. It has been a pleasure to work with your organisation over the last few years and we hope that prices will improve to such an extent as will justify the reopening of the mine.

Yours faithfully,

W. Blair, Director.

At the beginning of 1958 the Manager, Arnold Taylor, had been replaced by H. A. Smith, previously mine captain, but who was now only accorded the title of 'Acting' Manager. As things were grinding to a halt during the summer of 1958 Smith made every effort to interest the ultimate proprietors, Johannesburg Consols, in keeping at least some of the team together at Parc - clearly hoping that prices might improve, and believing that if the nucleus of the work-force was kept together, there would be a much better prospect of the mine getting back into production.

The following is a brief summary of the correspondence between Smith and his London boss, J. B. Dennison.

June, 1958 — Smith to Dennison

Smith believed that Llanrwst Lead Mines may not have been paid an allowance for the germanium which might have been recovered from the zinc concentrates sent to Avonmouth. Such a premium might have made continued milling profitable. (There was certainly a measurable germanium content in the Parc mine ore, as had been disclosed when the Ministry of Fuel and Power had written to Llanrwst Mines some years previously. They had enquired about the possibility of germanium being present, but, having been told that there was a trace, they were evidently not sufficiently impressed with the values to pursue the matter.)

Smith went on to suggest that if the mill is not to be employed producing lead and zinc concentrates for some time, then it could be used to contribute to a scheme to recover ferrous material from the tailings. He calculated that it would be possible to extract 32.5 tons of ferrous material each twenty-four hours from 500 tons of tailings, making use of a flotation process. If the resultant material contained 60% ferrous sulphide it would be marketable.

Dennison's reply dismissed the possibility of a possible germanium premium, and also dismissed the 'ferrous' scheme on the grounds that the extraction process would be too costly. Smith wrote again during the same month saying that assay laboratory trials indicated that if the remaining zinc was extracted prior to pyrites recovery, the process became economically viable. He asked Dennison to consider the following -

PROJECT - To extract zinc and pyrites from over 500,000 tons of tailings.

Advantages to the Company —

1)   Continued operation from the mine.
2)   Revenue to offset mining costs.
3)   Retention of specialised personnel for such time as it became economic to resume production of lead and zinc concentrates.
4)   Reduction of size of dump by 6%.
5)   Covering of caretaking costs if a temporary pause proved necessary in development work in the mine.

Dennison replied to Smith that the profit from the scheme, if it could be realised as projected, would still not cover the cost of continuing mine development.

July, 1958 - Smith to Dennison

He was still optimistic about the possibilities with the pyrites, he was also trying the Cyffty dumps.

If the pyrites price was not attractive would Dennison consider a further scheme to market the silica sand content of the tailings?

Dennison replied that the silica sand had been offered before to no avail. However, he did ask for an assay of the tailings, as there was a possibility of selling material to Courtaulds to supply their sulphuric acid manufacturing plant at Greenfield.

Smith to Dennison - as the mill is now available, it is possible to eliminate the problem which had prohibited the sale of silica sand previously.

He also sent Dennison an assay certificate claiming 48.5% sulphur in the tailings sample provided.

Dennison was now sufficiently impressed to authorise a full scale experiment, but with independent assayists. He instructed Smith to retain the necessary men for a further two weeks and to thoroughly clean the plant in preparation for the test. Everything had to be optimal, as Courtaulds required a 48% sulphur content before they would consider doing business.

August, 1958 - Smith to Dennison - on forwarding the Report.

'I am afraid the Report reads like a post-mortem.'

There had been several mechanical problems, but - worst of all - the assay results were only 45-46% sulphur. However, Smith believed that results of 46-8% sulphur could be achieved.

Dennison replied to Smith - '- the results are, of course, a great disappointment.'

September, 1958 - Smith to Dennison.

Smith had approached the Associated Ethyl Company to offer them the stockpile of twenty-one tons of pyrites for their bromine plant in Anglesey. They may be prepared to purchase some pyrites over the next few months, as long as it contained 46% sulphur, but at the end of that time they were changing their process to use sulphur rather than pyrites.

Dennison was non-committal about this project, but he did provide Smith with details of the Miller Separator, which was a gravity table, and which Smith welcomed as the answer to the problem of separating minerals and silica sand from the tailings.

This file in the Company records holds no further correspondence between the two men, and it may be fair to assume that they felt that they had now explored all possibilities for commercial exploitation of the dumps. The mill was to have a brief renaissance during the early 1960s, when it was used in an experiment on the automated control of mineral processing, but before discussing that episode, we will examine both mining operations and the Parc mill in more detail.

PARC MINE

A Ball Mill in the course of being crated for shipment to Nigeria.

Ore Wagons, etc., also waiting to be taken away when the mine closed finally at the beginning of the 1960s.

PARC MINE

The derelict mine buildings during the 1960s.

The portal of the No. 3, or Haulage Level, at the same time – gated and with the rails taken up.

METHODS OF MINING ADOPTED AT PARC DURING THE 1950s

Prior to Llanrwst Mines tenure of Parc the traditional techniques of overhanded and under-handed stoping had been quite adequate - however, as requirements at the mill were stepped up by the new company, so it became necessary to find ways of increasing output of ore from the mine.

Being an offshoot of an international company, who were fully up-to-date in their methods - witness the diamond drilling programme prior to opening the mine - it was not long before Parc underground was being comprehensively modernised.

Peter Gray described mining methods which were employed in Parc during his time as Manager, and Figures 24 and 25 illustrate these techniques.

One significant change was made when a new No.3 intermediate, or haulage level, was driven in the footwall of the Principal lode. From this new level connections were driven the few feet across to the old No.3 level, which had been driven in the lode, and Eimco loaders, or rocker shovels, carried the ore through these connections to be loaded into tubs in the haulage level. This had the effect of separating stoping and haulage, which led to greater ease and efficiency of working.

From an early stage they stopped hauling ore from the No.2 level, but carried it in side-tipping wagons to ore chutes which discharged into the stopes above the No.3 level, from where it was hauled with the ore from these stopes. However, this movement of ore within the No.2 level was considered to be expensive and inefficient, and the management hit on a smart idea to overcome this problem.

> Dennison visited Parc mine late in 1955, when he commented as follows -
> *'An ingenious moveable chute has been devised for the transfer of ore from the stopes above the No.2 level into the stopes above the No.3 level which is resulting in a welcome cut in costs.'*

They had achieved the trick by sinking connection shafts at the side of the No.2 level beneath the ore chutes from the stopes above that level. The

Fig. 24

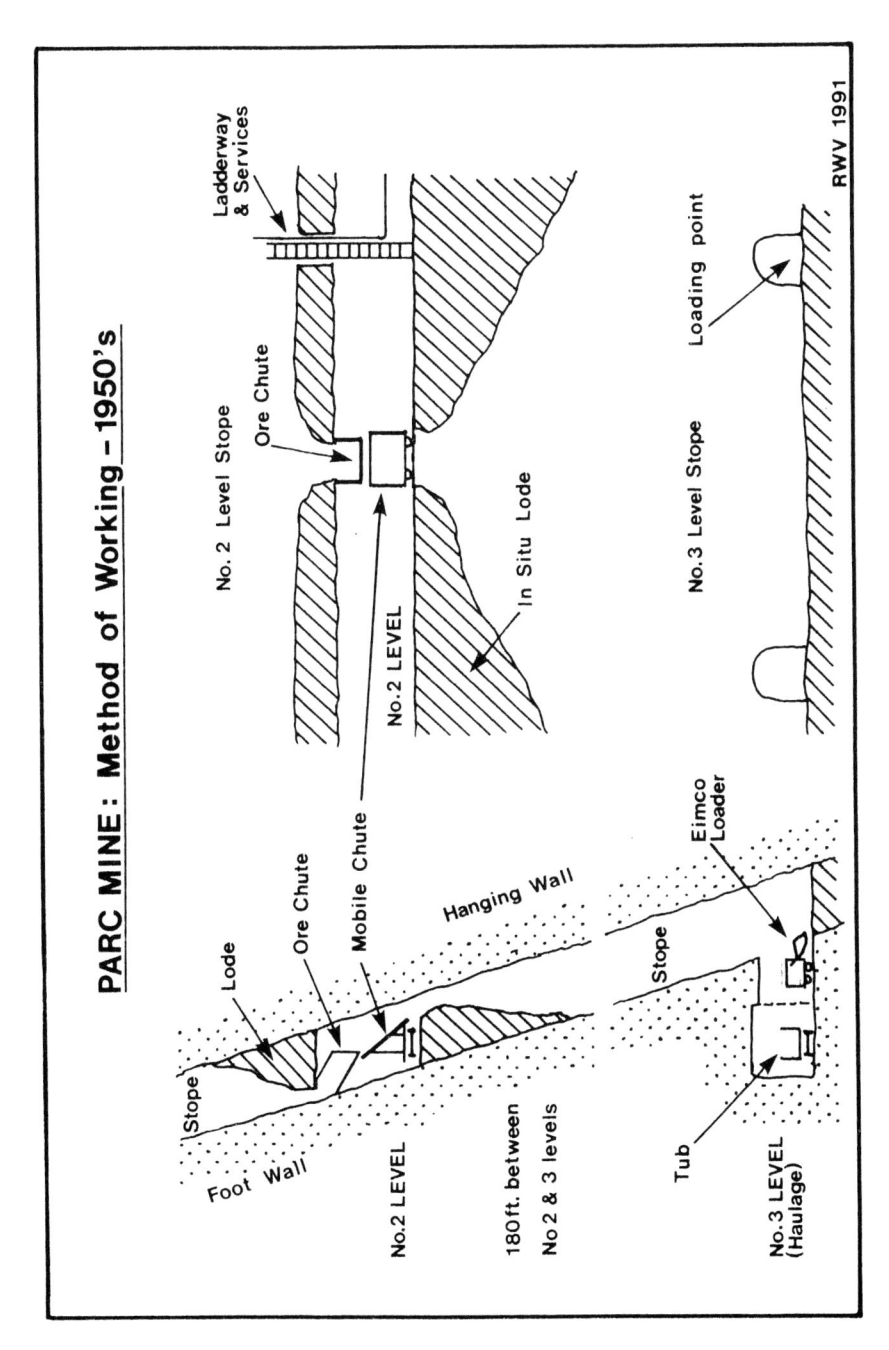

moveable chute was an inclined steel trough mounted on a mine car chassis, which could be moved from ore chute to ore chute on the No.2 level. When these chutes were opened the ore was directed by this contrivance into the shaft which fed it into the stopes above the No.3 level - hence to the haulage level. The moveable chute is seen in situ in the diagram Figure 24, which graphically illustrates the whole process as described above. It is also in situ in the mine - hidden away somewhere in the westerly reaches of the No.2 level - where it is likely to stay.

The actual removal of the material from the lode was achieved by overhanded stoping above both No.2 and No.3 levels, and Gray's lecture included a description of the shrinkage stoping which was employed in some parts of the mine.

The lode was divided into blocks 250ft. in length, and the procedure employed in delineating the material to be stoped, and the stoping sequence, is illustrated in Figure 25. The effect of keeping a floor between the level and the stope drive was to create what were, in effect, a series of underground ore bins in the stope, from which ore could be drawn as required. As long as the miners had a good 'start' on the mill operatives, there was always a reserve of broken ore to hand.

To the west of Gorlan they altered their technique to some extent, when they employed 'Christmas tree rises' to block out the stope in the first instance. Here they put up rises every 500ft., from which short sub-levels were driven each 12ft. The rises served as ladderways and pipe connections, needing no timbering, while the broken ore in the stopes was kept out of the rise by the pillars between the sub-levels.

Not the least important 'revolution' which occurred at Parc mine when Llanrwst Mines took over was the erection of a mill which was capable of coping with a much greater throughput than any of its predecessors, and which at last took account of twentieth century advances in the treatment of metallic ores. This mill is descibed in the following section.

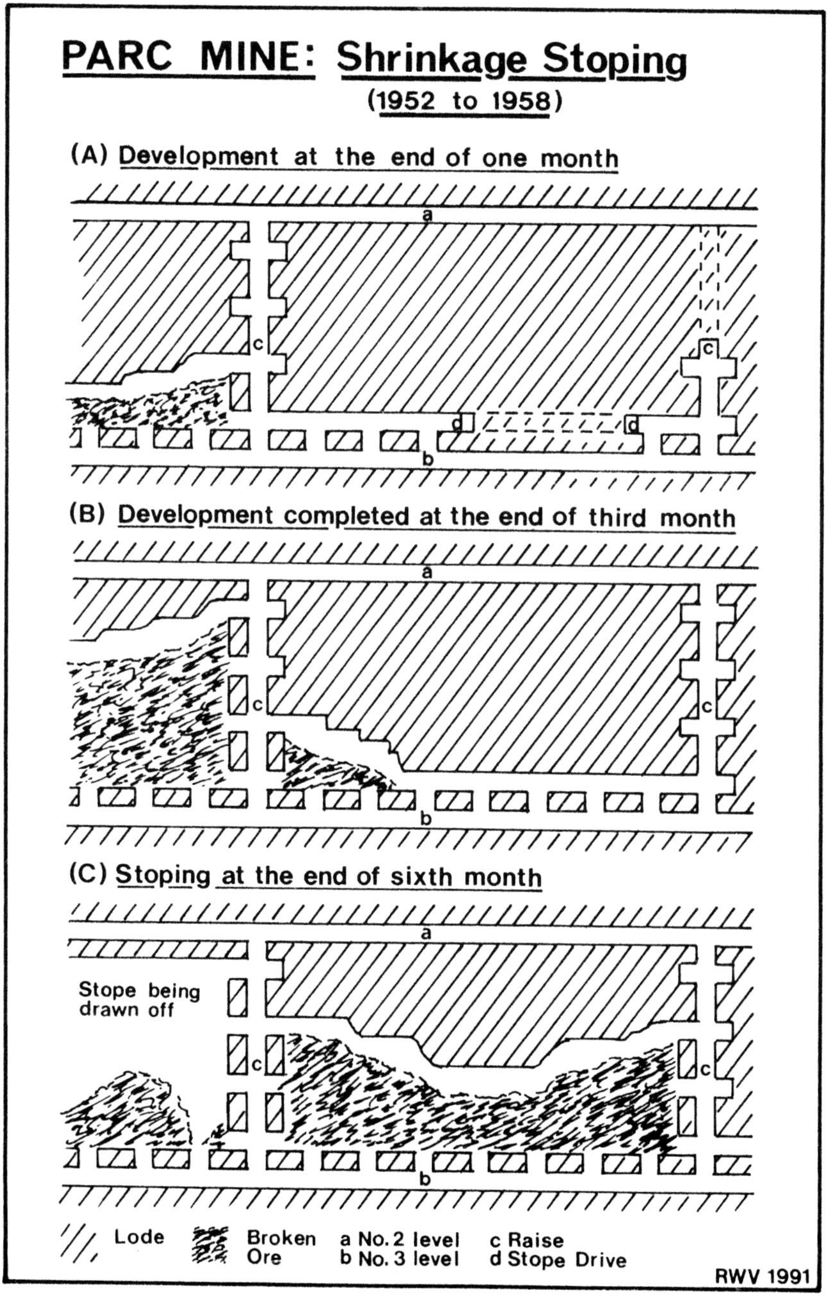
PARC MINE: Shrinkage Stoping
(1952 to 1958)
(A) Development at the end of one month
a
c
c
d
d
b
(B) Development completed at the end of third month
a
c
c
b
(C) Stoping at the end of sixth month
a
Stope being drawn off
c
c
b
Lode
Broken Ore
a No. 2 level
b No. 3 level
c Raise
d Stope Drive
RWV 1991

Fig. 25

THE PARC MINE MILL DURING THE 1950s

From foregoing descriptions it can be seen that from the time of D'Eresby Mountain, who erected one waterwheel to drive a crusher and a second to run jigs, the story of mineral dressing at Parc mine had been one of gradual improvement to a basic gravity technique, and this held true up to 1940, when the last and most sophisticated equipment was installed by the Watende Co. However, with the installation of flotation plant in the 1952 mill, the Llanrwst Mines Company finally brought Parc right up to date.

This new and modern equipment was erected by R. O. Stokes & Co. Ltd., who were also the principal manufacturers. A flow chart, explaining the progress of the ore through the mill, is seen in Figure 26, and the increased expectation for production is indicated by the capacity of the ore bin, which been has increased from the sixty tons of the earlier mill to five hundred tons in the new.

The object of the mill was to separate the metal sulphides - lead and zinc - from the vein material in which it was held, so producing what are termed as 'concentrates'. It should be remembered that the 'ore' when it first reached the mill actually consists of over ninety per cent gangue, or waste material - at least that was so at the Parc mine. At its simplest, the ore from the mine, with its very substantial impurity, was crushed virtually to a pulp, when the concentrated ore and the gangue materials were separated by a chemical process.

So - as one may follow on the diagram in Figure 26 - the ore first passed over a 'grizzley', which is an inclined grating, and which permitted any pieces of material up to three inches in dimension to pass through to the next stage.

Material which did not pass through the grating went to a jaw crusher, a powerful machine, which works in the way that it sounds as though it should, by crushing ore between a fixed, upright, vertical jaw and a moveable jaw, the size of the crushed material being determined by the separation of the jaws at their lowest point. From this machine the pieces of ore are returned small enough to be allowed to pass to the second stage of the process.

The ore now passed through much the same proceedure once again, though on this occasion the reduction in size is from up to three inches to no more than half an inch. This was achieved by passing it over a Nordberg rod deck screen, which allowed the smaller pieces to pass through, being assisted in this function by continuous vibration of the screen. The larger pieces which failed to pass through the screen at the first attempt are carried on to a Symons cone crusher, where they were sufficiently reduced to pass through the screen at their second attempt. The cone crusher consists of a crushing head gyrating inside a stationary concave crushing surface, and is able to effect a reduction in size of the pieces of ore by a factor of ten.

Before setting out on the next stage the ore went to the fine ore bin, which had a capacity of two hundred and fifty tons.

During the early days of milling at Parc the management employed three or four boys to pick waste rock as the ore moved between the grizzley and the screen, when they were able to pick as much as one hundred and fifty tons of rock each month. This was something of a throw-back to the early, labour intensive methods, and when they became more confident of the capabilities of the mill they decided that this sorting was not necessary.

From the fine ore bin the material went to two ball mills for further reduction, the mills being 'looped' with two rake classifiers to ensure that the reduction in the size of the fragments of ore was adequate before allowing it to go on to its next destination in the flotation cells. The ball mills were simply large horizontal rotating cylinders, containing numbers of steel balls. The movement of the steel balls in the mill as it rotated pulverised the ore. The material then went to the rake classifiers - basically combs, or rakes, which separated out any particles which were larger than '60 mesh' size. This is a fraction less than one thousandth of an inch in diameter, which was the maximum allowed to go forward to the flotation cells. Any larger particles were returned to the ball mills for further attention.

The flotation technique has already been met in this series of volumes on the Gwydyr mines, having been mentioned when introduced at Hafna during the years immediately before the first world war - a long time before it reached Parc. It depends on causing the slurry of pulped ore to froth, when chemical conditioning can cause particular metal ions to be attracted to the surface of the bubbles. This much concentrated material may then be collected from the surface of the cells.

At Parc they used a reagent called 'Aerofloat' in the lead flotation cells, which caused frothing and also collected lead ions. While this part of the

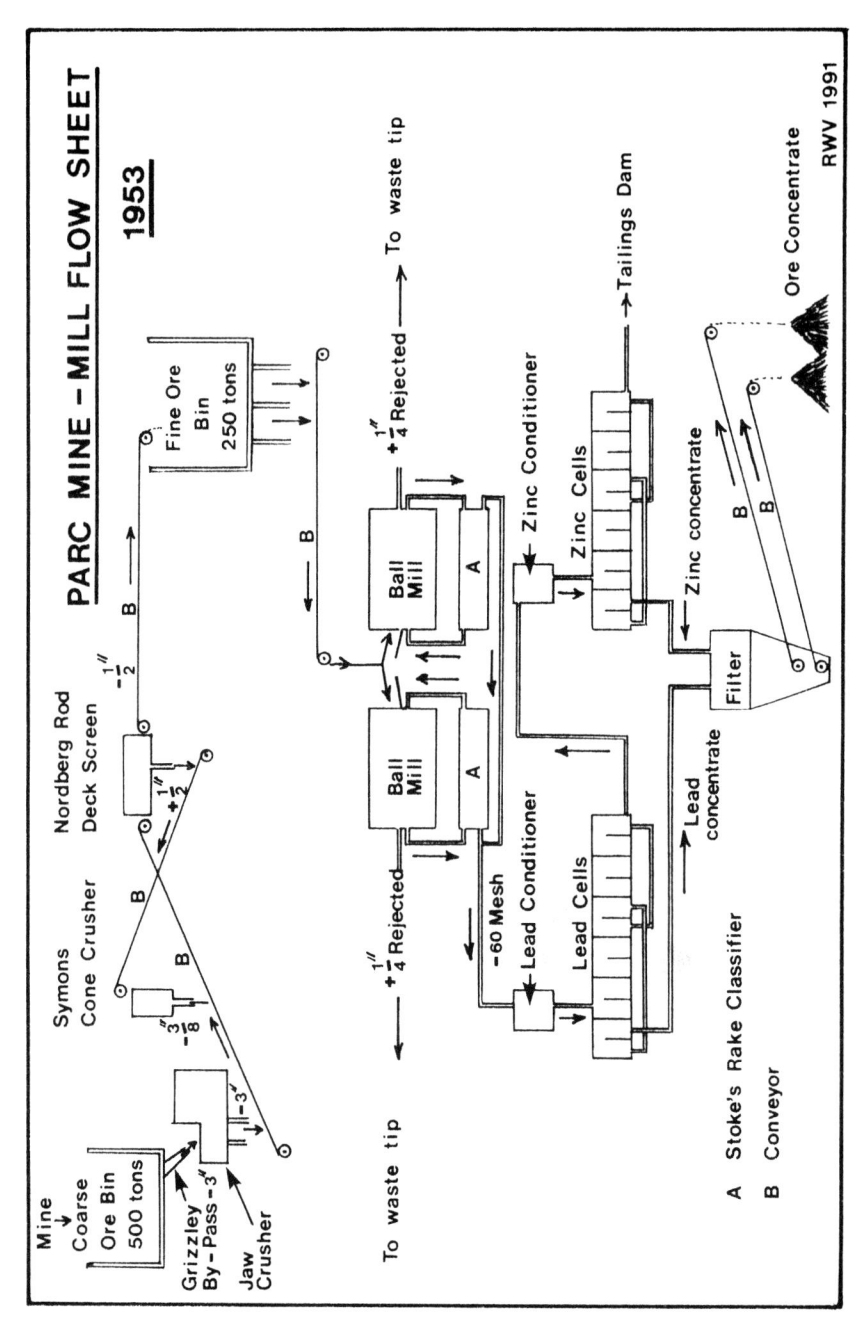

Fig. 26

process took place they added zinc sulphate to depress the activity of the zinc content of the pulp - which was a description of the pulverised ore and reagent as they had now become - and sodium silicate, which depressed the silica content. When the lead had been extracted they re-activated the zinc content of the slurry with the addition of copper sulphate. Pine oil was added as a 'frother' and potassium ethyl xanthate as a collecting agent. In this case it was necessary to depress the activity of the pyrite content, which was achieved by adding lime to the cell contents. They also employed sodium cyanide to depress the pyrite during some part of the time that this mill was at work. After completing the flotation process the concentrated ore was filtered, dried and bagged ready to be sent to the smelters.

At the outset of milling the management had defined certain levels of performance which they believed had to be maintained to allow profitable operation.

Their initial expectation as regards to throughput was for 210 tons per day, which was to employ three shifts of men working for six days each week. This was soon found to be too optimistic, and it was necessary to shut down at a very early stage to make adjustments to the flotation cells and to arrange the ball mills to be run in parallel. However, even with these changes they were only able to achieve one hundred and fifty tons a day during the early stages. However, as they grew in experience, they were able to increase these figures substantially, reaching over three hundred tons a day by 1955. Indeed, during the latter stages of the operation they were able to talk of reaching a maximum of four hundred and fifty tons per day, though it does not seem likely that they actually reached this target.

A second factor which was essential to success was that they should be feeding the mill with 'payable ore'. To measure this they devised a criterion which was described as the 'lead equivalent' of the ore. This made allowance for the added value which was given to the ore by its zinc content. The percentage of zinc was divided by three, and this was added to the percentage of lead in the ore, the resultant figure being the 'lead equivalent. The minimum acceptable aggregate total for profitable treatment was believed to be 5%, which could have been made up by 5% lead or 15% zinc, or any combination which added up to the same -however, by 1956, they were prepared to carry on milling ore with as little as 4.55% lead equivalent. This may have been because they had been able to achieve higher than expected through-put of ore per day by then.

PARC MINE

The Flotation Cells at work. The conditioning tanks at the head of each bank of cells can just be detected in the background.

PARC MINE

The Dual Concentrates Filter – made by Eimco. The dark cake is lead sulphide, or galena, and the light cake is zinc sulphide, or sphalerite.

PARC MINE

Concentrates being loaded onto a road haulage vehicle. Lead concentrates were taken by road to the Associated Lead Manufacturer's smelter at Chester, and the zinc concentrates were sent by rail from Llanrwst to Swansea.

The third consideration was that they should produce concentrates which were sufficiently high in metal content, and which did not contain any impurities that might make them unacceptable to the smelters.

As far as lead concentrates were concerned, the initial aim was to achieve a metal content of 84%, though they were not able to get anywhere near this during the early months. However, after the adjustments were made to the ball mills and the flotation cells they did find themselves able to attain 80% to 81% - provided that they obeyed three cardinal rules -

i)   there must be a 4% minimum lead ore in the mill feed,

ii) there must be continuous operation of both ball mills, and

iii) the reagent feeders to the flotation cells must ensure a twenty-four hour process.

This still left them having to overcome an initial problem with 3.8% silica in the concentrate, which exceeded the 2% maximum allowed by the smelters. This was apparently a question of ensuring adequate suppression during the flotation process

In contrast to this, there was no problem at all with the zinc concentrates, where the 55% to 60% attained was quite satisfactory.

One last problem existed as far as the mill was concerned, and it was not a new one at Parc - this was the provision of an adequate supply of water to enable them to keep the process going. The principal source was a 3ins. main from Llyn y Parc, which descended the air shaft, and then travelled along the No.3 level to the mill. Elsewhere water was taken from the Cilstent level, the old No.1 level, and from the Nant Uchaf reservoir. With these various sources they were evidently able to keep up with the demand.

After the concern was halted by unfavourable returns on their ore sales in 1958, they placed both the mine and the mill on a 'care and maintainance' basis, which meant that they were easily accessible for an experiment undertaken by the Department of Scientific and Industrial Research in 1962 and 1963, for which a mill and supply of ore was required. This is briefly described below.

DEPARTMENT OF SCIENTIFIC & INDUSTRIAL RESEARCH PARC MINE EXPERIMENT, 1962-3.

This project was conceived in 1960, by the Mineral Processing Division of the DSIR, which was based at the Warren Springs Laboratory. Their object was defined as '- seeking to obtain basic information required for the application of automatic control to mineral treatment processes and to indicate any modification to existing equipment and instruments which may be necessary to achieve automation'.

The decision was made to use a small full-scale plant, as this would offer much greater opportunity for realistic appraisal under the varying conditions which were met in real life - rather than risking the incipient errors which arose from scaling-up laboratory experiments. Parc mine, which contains ample ore for a sustained run of the mill, was an excellent candidate, as the mill itself exhibited a typical range of dressing machinery, which - as mentioned above - had been kept on 'care and maintainance' since milling stopped there in 1958.

To oversee the project the DSIR requested the National Research Development Council to form a project committee, and to seek the technical assistance of E-A Automation Systems in designing the experiment. Representatives of several of the large mining houses sat on this committee, including Peter Gray, who had only stepped down as manager of this mine in 1956. He formally represented the owners of the Parc mine, who were by then described as Hawkswick Investments Ltd., evidently some part of the Johannesburg Consols empire. In the event it was Gray who was put in charge of all practical matters in the mine.

The modifications to the mill were described as not being of a major nature, though they did include changes in the feed system to the cone crusher, partitioning of the fine ore bin, and replacement of the rake classifier with a cyclone. The thickening tanks, which had been by-passed from an early stage in the 1950s mill, were re-connected, a re-grinding circuit was introduced to permit variation of particle size entering the zinc flotation part of the process, and the reagent feed system was modified.

In the mine itself, after necessary preparatory work in bringing the equipment, locomotives, pumps, etc., to working readiness, and after having cleared the levels and diverted excessive volumes of water which were entering the workings from the Cyffty Western shaft, the men were able to start mining by the May of 1962.

They anticipated that they would need twenty weeks to establish the required constant flow of ore which needed to be available before the mill was started, and in total - including the period after the mill was working - they were mining for a little over six months between May and November of 1962. During this time they broke something in the order of 20,000 tons of ore.

This was taken from several points in the mine. In the first case stoping above the No.2 and No.3 levels, and subsequently from the Reservoir lode. A brief essay on the Hafna lode came to a rapid halt, when they broke into unknown and water-filled early workings.

Some idea of what they were achieving physically may be made from the report made in December 1962, at which time they had spent 964 hours milling 4408 tons of ore, and had produced 70 tons of lead concentrate and 46 tons of zinc concentrate. This would translate into a modest thirty to forty tons per shift, with an even more modest 'lead equivalent' of less than two. However, profitable mining was not the exercise, though these results must have made it easy for Hawkswick Investments to do as they did, allowing the lease to lapse immediately after the experiment had been concluded.

An official spokesman had this to say about the undertaking - 'This project will not lead directly to automation of mineral processing, but it will reveal information that will form a basis for future development. If it is successful it will give automation engineers in this country a lead over the rest of the world.'

When the last of the ore was milled in February of 1963, the experiment was dismantled, and the buildings were very soon sold by Hawkswick Investments to the Forestry Commission - however, it is a pleasing thought that the last effort in Parc may still be contributing to the success of mining operations throughout the rest of the mining world!

In fact Parc mine did have one more contribution to make, though not in the mining field, which was when it became the home of the Bidston Experiment.

THE BIDSTON TIDAL EXPERIMENT - 1968

At this time the Bidston Tidal Institute were seeking confirmation of the results of experiments which they had been conducting in their laboratory in Bidston. Basically they were looking for ways of measuring the tilting of the coastal strip which occurred due to the alteration of weight off-shore as the tide came in and went out. To obtain their results they needed a secure and undisturbed environment, at an appropriate distance from the coast, and in Parc mine they were able to fulfil all these requirements.

A section of the No.2 level to the east of the Gors lode was partitioned off, in which an Askania vertical pendulum and a Verbaandert-Melchoir pendulum were housed, while the recording equipment was placed in the fan house - allowing the connecting cables to run down the air shaft. The results of the experiments were the fount of several learned papers and a good deal of controversy. However, they were eventually recognised as being of critical importance in this field, as they were used to demonstrate that the results of tiltmeter experiments performed in tunnels could not be relied upon, as they were subject to distortion in relation to the excavated cavity in which they stood. Not very good news to the fifty or so other 'tunnel' experimenters across the world, some of whom had drilled their cavities at great expense.

PARC MINE IN RECENT YEARS

The first of the visible remains to go from the Parc sett were the buildings. None of the nineteenth century stone constructions, dressing floors or waterwheel pits which are found elsewhere in Gwydyr survived the reconstruction which accompanied Llanrwst Mines tenure during the 1950s. The recent structures were principally corrugated iron, and they were dismantled during the years after the Forestry Commission acquired the sett in 1963.

Well and away the most substantial artefacts were, of course, the tailings dumps, covering many acres in the valley below the mine buildings and in the Nant Uchaf lagoon to the west. The latter, comprising some 170,000 tons, was thought more of a problem, and Llanrwst Mines did make some effort to beautify the area by planting willows and birches. And they did turn out to be a problem, when, in 1964, a flash flood broke through into the workings on the

Reservoir lode and carried great volumes of water and mine waste through the mine and discharged them out of the adit on the main haulage level. This, in turn, carried very substantial waste from the tip below the mine down to the main road in the valley and the fields beyond.

Not until 1977 were the physical and aesthetic problems created by these tips dealt with in any comprehensive manner. In that year a grant from the Welsh Development Agency allowed the Snowdonia National Park authority to take all necessary steps to stabilise the main tailings dump below the mine, by diverting the Nant Gwyd stream, and by capping old shafts on the No.5 level. As a part of this approach the dump was graded and grassed over, which gives it the bland appearance that it now presents.

However, the upper tailing dump had resisted camouflage to a large extent, and was again attracting anxious attention by the end of the 1980s, though more on account of its contents than its appearance. The options now seemed to be either to remove it, or to encase it in a plastic envelope, to prevent pollution of the Conwy river by the water which was passing through the waste on its way down the Nant. In the event both these courses of action were too expensive, and a further planting programme is under consideration.

Inside the mine the last thirty years have seen a steady deterioration in conditions, with rotting timbers and a series of minor earthquakes in the area leading to collapse in the stopes. What was a favourite site among mine explorers and archaeologists, especially as Parc had unwatered older mines in the area and afforded underground access to them, has now become unstable and unsafe. In particular, at the point where the Gorlan lode displaced the Principal lode - already mentioned above - falls have led to a blockage, behind which it is feared that a dangerous weight of water might collect. To obviate any serious flooding which might occur should this blockage give way and release a large volume of water, a choke dam has been constructed in the No.3 level a short distance to the south of Kneebone's cutting. At the same time all shafts and adits in the mine have been sealed, and the mine can no longer be entered.

PARC MINE

The Tailings Pond below the Mill. The pond was self-constructing, when the tailings pulp was discharged from the peripheral pipe system, coarse particles settled first and were heaped to form a baulk around the edge of the pond.

A later view of the tailings after they had been landscaped and sown with grass.

PARC MINE

Parc No. 3 level photographed many years after mining had ceased.

The top of the Parc Underground Shaft at the same date as the above.

THE MINES AS THEY ARE TODAY

Parc Mine: Strangely, in light of its relative size and importance, the Parc mine has left few remains other than the landscaped dumps and gated adits.

To get the best view of what does remain, one should make a start from the bottom of the old mine road which leaves the Nant road a little to the south of Nant Cottage. If you are parking a car you will find a number of casual parking spaces hereabouts, but please try not to block passing places or Forestry Commission gates !! Figure 27 will be helpful in understanding the following notes.

The mine road passes uphill in a southerly direction, and the landscaped tailings are obvious on ones right hand. After a few hundred yards of walking you will be able to see two entrances at the head of the tailings. The lower of these is the No.4 adit entrance, and the brickwork which you will see was almost certainly put in place by Messrs. Brunner Mond around the turn of the century.

The higher, concrete adit entrance was constructed during the 1950s by Llanrwst Mines Limited. This is the No.3 level entrance, and was the main haulage level. There is no remnant of the substantial mill buildings which stood here until the 1960s.

A few yards beyond and above the No.3 adit entrance one may walk onto a fenced area above this adit. If you look to your left as you walk onto this area you will be able to tell from the lie of the land that there may be some sort of a hole twenty or thirty yards away. There is. Do not climb over to see ! This is Kneebone's Cutting, and it is very dangerous to approach the edge, though, if plans which are afoot come to fruition, by the time you are reading this there may be a safe walk-way available to look down into the cutting.

Walking on up the mine road you will soon come to a track leading off to your right. If you follow this you will soon see the Nant Uchaf tailing lagoon though the trees on your right hand side. This covers an extensive area, and again it is not a safe place, as there are currently open stopes at the south west corner, which communicate with deep workings in the Parc mine itself.

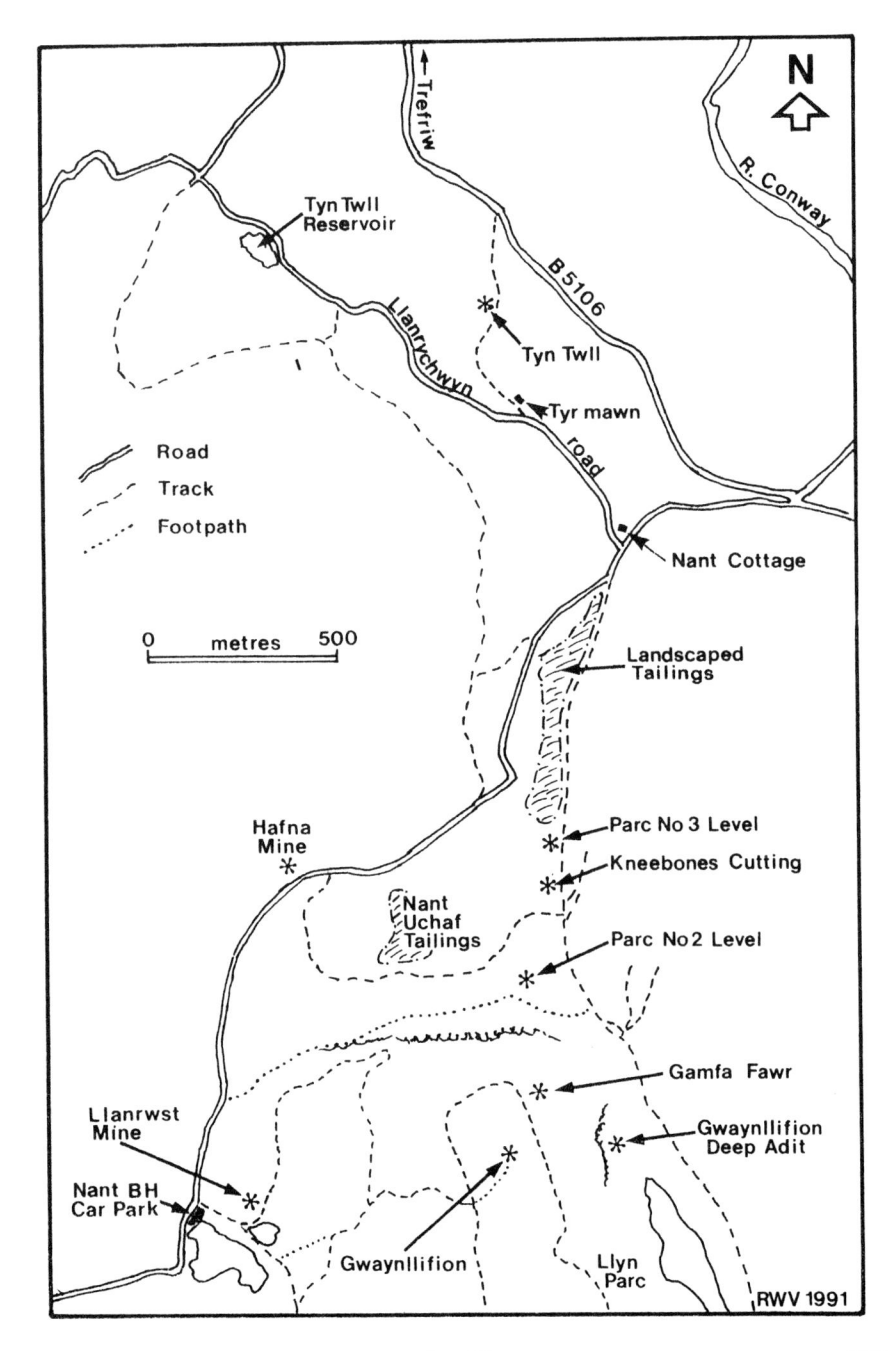

Fig. 27

Returning to the mine road and proceeding a little further up the hill, you will very soon come to another track on your right hand side. This may be followed into a small clearing - passing a capped shaft on the Parc mine Gors lode - and the No.2 adit entrance may be found diagonally across the clearing to your right. This has also been sealed. Beyond this there are few artefacts which could be said to relate to Parc itself, though the Powder Magazine, seen among the photographs overleaf, is a striking exception. However, in the forest all around there is much evidence that a great deal of open stoping and digging of minor shafts and trials must have taken place in the area.

Tyn Twll (Clementina) Mine: As with the walk to Parc mine, the best spot to start from, if you are parking a car, is in the region of the Nant Cottage - again you will be assisted by Figure 27. You should set out along the Llanrhychwyn road, which forks right off the Nant road immediately beyond the cottage. Very soon on your right hand you will be able to make out something of the Grey Mare's Tail waterfall, which is on the Park Mawr - an old area of mining trials - none of which came to anything, and none of which are now approachable.

A short distance further up the Llanrhychwyn road you will find the entrance to Tyr Mawn. If you leave the road at this point you will find a track which passes along the west side of Tyr Mawn and then enters a wooded area. In wet weather you will find that you cross more than one minor ford along this path, but when you reach the most substantial of them - distinguished by the stone walling on your left hand side, which marks out the water-course, you have reached the area of greatest interest.

During the first half of the nineteenth century Tyn Twll reported in association with ventures at Tyr Mawn, which we have passed, Llety, which you would find higher up the Llanrhychwyn road, and Rhydloew. As mentioned before, it seems very possible that this old ford may well be the rhyd (or ford) of Rhydloew.

When you have crossed this ford the tenement of Tyn Twll lies directly on your right hand. If you look across the fence at this point you will see that the water which flowed across the ford used to be collected by an old stone-lined watercourse. From here it was carried by leat to turn the waterwheel near the Roadside shaft at the side of Tyn Twll house. The pit for this wheel still exists, as do very much ruined remains of the structure which held the larger wheel subsequently erected by the Clementina company during the latter half of the nineteenth century - however, this land is strictly private, and should be treated accordingly.

If you walk some hundred yards down the track beyond the ford, you will be able to detect the outline of the Clementina Mine buildings in the forest to your left. Again it must be stressed that these buildings are on Forestry Commission land, and are in a dangerous state.

Beyond the mine buildings the track carries down to the main road near to the Pant y Carw quarry. Returning to the Llanrhychwyn road, the Tyn Twll reservoir may be discerned some distance up this road, on the left hand side.

Gwaynllifion: If you are walking from your car, the best starting place is from the Nant B.H. car park at the side of Llyn Sarnau - near to the restored Llanrwst engine house at the top of the Nant. From here you leave the road on the Forestry Commission track which passes to the south of the engine house. The most direct route takes you along the footpath which can be seen on the map heading ENE after you have crossed the causeway, and which takes you alongside the Alltwen mine - already described in the first volume of this series.

If you climb this path - which is very neglected - you will first of all meet one track, which you cross keeping up the hill and carrying on ENE - then you will emerge onto a another track - which takes you on up the hill into a fair sized clearing. If you look at the map you will see that you could have reached this point by taking this track where it bore left immediately after you had passed the engine house and crossed the causeway - a good deal further to walk, but a good deal drier if the undergrowth is wet.

From the clearing there is an obvious path leading east, which you may follow onto the High Plateau. As you step onto this path you will notice quite substantial surface workings and shafts on your right hand, which are on the outcrop of the Bryn Eisteddfod lode.

When you reach a junction after a short walk, you will emerge onto another Forestry track - when you will have just passed the surface workings on the Cobbler's lode - and are now entering on Gwaynllifion proper. The path now crosses the Forestry track which you have just reached - slightly to the right as you cross - and becomes less marked.

After a short distance you will encounter an area of extensive working. The first waste heaps are those around a group of shafts which were sunk in the

THE LEAD MILL STREAM

The Nant Gwyd stream in the vicinity of the Felin Blwm. Below this point a canal to the River Conwy at Trefriw was commenced sometime at the end of the nineteenth century.

Photograph by Brian Jones.

PARC MINE

The Powder Magazine near to the Parc No. 2 adit entrance.
Photograph by Brian Jones.

PARC MINE

The Parc No. 2 adit entrance thirty years after the mine was closed.
Photograph by Brian Jones.

GWAYNLLIFION

One of the group shafts in the region of the intersection of the Gwaynllifion Deep Adit and the New Lode.

Photograph by Brian Jones.

region of the intersection of Sutton's lode and the New lode, where the proprietors had elected to sink their engine shaft to the Gwaynllifion deep adit during the 1860s.

Beyond these you will discover the remains of the mine buildings, and the dressing floors - such as they were - and you will now see ahead of you the very extensive surface workings of Owen's lode. These runs away in a northerly direction towards the Coed y Fucheslas escarpment.

Beyond this point, while there is a footpath on the maps, the way is not at all clear, and care must be taken if you wish to proceed. If you should do so, and continuing in an easterly direction, you will soon find yourself on the Forestry track which you crossed on entering Gwaynllifion, as it has completed a 180 degree turn to the north to come back in front of you again.

If you turn left on reaching the track on this second occasion, and walk to the north until the track is about to swing west, you will be opposite to the Gamfa Fawr sett, which is only a short distance on your right hand.

Since the survey described in this volume was made in 1985 the landowners have seen fit to bulldoze this area, which has led to the almost complete destruction of one of the oldest and most unusual sites in the Gwydyr Forest - however, it is still possible to find the knockstone and rudimentary shelter wall, which gave a minimal amount of protection to those who were hand dressing ore on this site generations ago, and also the bare area of rock which is believed to have been a simple dressing floor.

REFERENCES AND MAP REFERENCES

COMPANY RECORDS: Public Records Office, Kew, London.

Clementina Mining Co. Ltd. BT/31/2275/10920

D'Eresby Consolidated Mining Co. Ltd. BT/31/2411/12112

D'Eresby Mountain Mining Company BT/31/2313/11213

D'Eresby Mining Company BT/31/3376/20175

D'Eresby & Gwydir Mines Ltd. BT/31/4705/31009

Gwydyr Amalgamated Mining Co. BT/31/2764/15063

Gwydyr Park Consols Mining Co. BT/31/1547/4956

Llanrwst Consolidated Mines BT/31/31998/98491

Parc Lead & Zinc Mining Co. BT/31/5636/39280

MINE PLANS

Parc Mine Plans - British Geological Survey, Aberystwyth and Caernarfon Record Office

Clementina Lead Mine   )
D'Eresby Mountain & Gwydyr   )
Parc and Fucheslas (1)   )   Caernarfon Record Office
Parc and Fucheslas (2)   )

GWYDYR ESTATE RECORDS:

Caernarfon Record Office
Lincoln Archive Office
Ancaster Estate Papers - (Private papers) Grimsthorpe Castle, Lincolnshire.
Collation Mines & Quarry Returns: Gwydyr Estate 1838-1920
J.S.Bennett & M.J.Lewis - deposited Clwyd & Gwynedd R.O.s

PRIVATE REPORTS:

Gwydyr Forest - Nant Uchaf. Report on the Mining Remains in the proposed Forest Park. R.W.Vernon, November 1986.

MISCELLANEOUS:

British Geological Survey Records: Aberystwyth.

Bulletin of the Geological Society of Great Britain, Vol.23. Lead and Zinc Ores in the Pre-Carboniferous Rocks of West Shropshire and North Wales, by Henry Dewey and Bernard Smith, 1922.

Mining Journal & Mining World - various from 1853.

Russell Bayles Parc Papers: Caernarvon Record Office.

Tidal Tilt at Llanrwst, North Wales: tidal loading and earth structure. T. F. Baker.

Geophys. J. R. Astro. Soc. (1980) 62, pp. 269-290.

Varvill Collection: Mining Dept., University of Leeds.

J. B. Dennison and W. W. Varvill. Prospecting with the diamond drill for lead-zinc ores in the British Isles. TIMM, Vol. 62, 1952-53. pp. 1-21.

A. A. Archer in 'The Future of Non-Ferrous Mining in Great Britain and Ireland'. IMM, 1959, pp. 259-276.

MAP REFERENCES:

Clementina Mine Crusher House (Tyn Twll)	SH/7862/6158
Clementina (Tyn Twll) Reservoir	SH/7803/6172
Felin Blwm	SH/7910/6110
Parc No.5 Adit (estimated)	SH/7880/6075
Parc No.4 Adit	SH/7874/6017
Parc No.3 Adit	SH/7877/6015
Parc No.2 Adit	SH/7868/5980
Kneebone's Cutting	SH/7874/6004
Parc Mine Magazine	SH/7874/5981
Parc Mine Air Shaft	SH/7879/5969
Gamfa Fawr	SH/7871/5951
Gwaynllifion Deep Adit	SH/7892/5936
Owen's Lode - Open Workings	SH/7863/5932
Cobbler's Lode - Open Workings	SH/7853/5920
Nant Uchaf Tailing Lagoon	SH/7840/5990
Fucheslas Deep Adit	SH/7863/6009

GLOSSARY

(This is an extension to the glossaries found in previous volumes)

CHATS – The "middlings" from jigging composed of ore and gangue which requires further crushing.

EIMCO – A Rocker Shovel used for loading ore into wagons underground.

GERMANIUM – An element usually found in zinc ores used in the manufacture of electronic components.

GRAVITY MILL – A mill in which separation of ore is carried out by the difference of Specific Gravity.

HARTZ or HARZ JIG – Common form of Jig consisting of two compartments. One contains the screens, the other a reciprocating plunger.

JAMES TABLE – Similar to a Wilfley Table.

JIGS – Method of separating ore and gangue of different specific gravities. finely crushed ore is agitated in a tank of water. Screens or sieves help to separate out the ore, the heaviest sinking to the bottom of the jig.

LAUNDER – A wooden trough used to convey water or a mixture of crushed ore and water in a mill.

MARCASITE – A form of iron pyrites.

TAILINGS – Waste material produced by milling.

TROMMEL – A rotating sieve or screen used for separating minerals by size.

VUGH – A cavity in a lode lined with crystals.

WILFLEY TABLE – A vibrating table which a mixture of finely crushed ore and gangue is streamed over. The process produces an ore concentrate with the waste or SAND going to the tailing lagoon.